Running Free

Running Free

June & Hal Miller

ZONDERVAN
PUBLISHING HOUSE
OF THE ZONDERVAN CORPORATION
GRAND RAPIDS, MICHIGAN 49506

RUNNING FREE

© 1977 by The Zondervan Corporation
Grand Rapids, Michigan

Library of Congress Cataloging in Publication Data
Miller, June.
    Running free.
    1. Success.   I. Miller, Hal, joint author.
II. Title.
BF637.S8M56   158'.1   76-55767

Printed in the United States of America

To

our four sons plus one

who have taught us many things

Contents

Preface

1 When You Can't Take Any More 13

2 The Why of Self 33

3 The How of Self. 47

4 Meeting the Different Ones. 65

5 The Gift Shop Is Open 79

6 From Natural to Supernatural Living. 89

7 How to Get the Spectacular Gifts 103

8 Free in the Family. 117

9 Free to Be Me 131

10 Depression-Proof Living. 151

11 Running Free 169

Preface

Have you ever had the feeling you were meant to be more than you are? More successful, happier, or of greater value to your world than you seem to be? Maybe you've grown a little bored and disgusted with trying and finding only small results or rebuffs and you've been thinking, "What's the use?"

But *trying* and *thinking* do not bring happiness or success. It is the discovery and use of something you have that nobody else in this world has that makes every impossibility you long for entirely possible. You have a special blend of temperament and natural talents *plus* a supernatural gift or gifts that provide everything you need to become a person you can respect and appreciate.

If you haven't discovered that gift yet, chances are your marriage is somewhat disillusioning if not a downright flop. If you have children, they probably bicker and periodically push you beyond your limits. If you are single, discovering your gift is especially important for it is the key to building worthwhile relationships that last beyond a few fleeting weeks or months.

Knowing your gift is like having a safety deposit box of unlimited tax-free wealth — not financial wealth, but resources to handle every life experience. The purpose of this book is to help you discover that gift and recognize the correlation of natural talents and temperament. It is to provide you with a handle to get hold of life itself and to have the power to get the most out of every situation and happening, whether good or bad, pleasant or difficult.

If you are working at a job you despise or find unsatisfying or if you are preparing for a career simply because it offers security and advancement — stop where you are! Pick up the key that unlocks your future. Find your gift and experience genuine satisfaction and a sense of self-worth in becoming the person you were uniquely designed and empowered to become.

So come into the gift shop, for it is never closed. Flip the page and browse with me as you consider a life of exciting fulfillment — a life where every dynamic part of your being moves smoothly forward in the harmony of becoming a greater you!

Running
Free

When You
Can't Take
Any More

Dear mom,

I hate myself for what I've done to you. I want to
see you, but I can't come home. If I did, we would only
fight again, and it just wouldn't work. Try to understand. . . .

Love,
Connie

Dear Tom and Christie,

I love you, but I must go away. I can't take things
the way they are. You'll be okay. You have your dad

and a nice home and plenty of money. Try to understand. . . .

Love,
Mom

What do you do when you can't take any more?

In a recent three-month period over 200,000 women who were wives and mothers were catalogued as "runaways." They had left home in search of an identity, a freedom and sense of fulfillment they did not find in their family relationships. During this same period of time countless young people and children were running away from parents, while husbands and fathers deserted their families.

But there is a happy alternative!

When the stress is greatest and we feel we must run . . . Run! There is no emotional freedom in running *from* the problem, for it shadows our steps with guilt, resentment, and fear of the future. But there can be a new beginning in running *to* the solution. We simply need to turn around and run in the right direction.

Problems are inner needs coming out in the open. Usually those needs are expressed in terms of conflict, and it is the conflict that exhausts us and ushers in the feeling, "I can't take any more. I've got to get away."

Our culture today has come through a time of radical change in most areas of life. We have watched and listened as men seethed in Watergate's juicy stew; women burned bras and pronounced themselves free; and in many hospital emergency rooms teen-agers were pronounced DOA. Newscasters spoke of liberation, but people were not freed from fear, worry, guilt, anguish, and disappointment.

Individual liberation transcends political corruption, releases new creativity under economic pressure, raises values in a declining market, heals broken marriages and rifts in parent-child relationships, and renews physical and mental health. It enables one to walk in unshaken security in a world of chaos and change. It creates profitable jobs when there are none and draws friends to warm themselves in the glow of a free life. It goes beyond external pressures and demands to identify the self that must face them all.

Millions have seen man's dilemma as if looking through a fractured windshield. Distorted, impractical, elusive solutions have been proposed, only to be discarded in the using. We have looked to the world and others to give us happiness, success, and fulfillment and have found that it is not out there.

Locked within every person is the embryonic seed of happy liberation, but in most lives it is crushed without their ever knowing of its existence. It is the secret of eliminating divorces, business failures, runaway children, teens, and parents, dirty politics, violence against the masses, and even suicide. The potential to identify and release this constructive power is within reach of everyone.

Something From the Past for the Future

Long ago a great Greek physician proposed a startling concept that has been buried under the avalanche of current psychological trivia. It is a key to current compulsions to run away or escape. Contrary to threadbare clichés, we are not what we are because of the influence of happenings of early childhood or later life, of places or people! We are what we are because of inner reactions and responses to those external impressions. Circumstances in themselves do not produce conflict nor do the actions and attitudes of others. It is the way we receive or reject these things that generates inward turmoil. The seeds of anxiety and depression germinate quickly in the humid climate of inward frustration and warfare of the mind and spirit.

Hippocrates rightly recognized that those reactions are greatly influenced by the temperament with which we are born, but he did not know the whole story. Individual temperaments are the soil out of which incredible power potential is fed. The latent seed is a God-given gift that is a personal passport to fulfillment. To understand temperaments without being able to recognize corresponding gifts and talents is like boarding a plane without an engine in anticipation of a transoceanic flight to adventure. The gift is the power plant that transforms natural energy into supernatural achievement, happiness, and liberation. It is this trio of temperament, talents, and supernatural gifts that largely determines how we feel about ourselves and others and how we react or respond to them and to circumstances in life.

For years our home was an emotional and psychological battleground. We fought and kissed until the kisses wore thin and the scars thickened. I searched for practical help and found none. I read books by the stack on subjects such as how to raise children. Most were nonsensical — they simply did not work in the nitty-gritty of daily living. I discovered that the "experts" who were loudly proclaiming, "Don't inhibit your children," were trying to salvage their own teen-agers from drugs, vandalism, hostility, and rebellion. Obviously they did not have effective answers, yet they were influencing vast numbers of parents.

During my search for solutions I discovered that most children's conflicts were blandly categorized as sibling conflicts, as if that term contained some magical explanation. The dictionary was helpful in reaffirming that sibling was a noun or adverb indicating one of two or more children or pertaining to a brother or sister. But that hardly solved my problem as to why these little darlings bit and hit and worked overtime at being and doing all that my children simply should not be or do.

Then one day, in a flash of incredible enlightenment, I began to realize that if my children were to be happy, they must have happy parents. Perhaps I would understand why my children had conflicts if I could solve the bigger mystery of why Hal and I had conflicts. I found an important part of that solution locked in the understanding of our temperaments and their effect upon each other. Much later I made the most important discovery of all — I found that God has given every person who has ever lived (and that includes me!) a highly personal supernatural gift that is the power source for practical living. That discovery sent me scurrying from the dark tunnel of failure out into the bright sunlight of freedom and personal identity. It has also propelled me along the road of proving in the laboratory of human experience (both mine and that of scores of other individuals) even the tiniest facet of these findings during the ensuing thirty years. This book has not evolved out of sterile test-tube concepts but out of the seething boiling pot of life that produces happiness and sorrow, bitterness and joy, laughter and tears. The crucible of human experience tends to discard senseless jargon and brings us head-on into reality.

But before we lift the veil that often hides the key we are searching for let's take a look at our total self.

Getting the Picture of Self in Focus

If we could strip away all the facade and accumulated cultural impact and get down to the basic person, we would instantly recognize that each of us is a three-dimensional being that is intended to be unified into a harmonious whole. That is, the physical body is the outer, visible revelation of the unseen inner person and is a necessary dimension for contact with the material world. The world knows us through our outward physical entity that expresses our inner person.

Our body is important to us, but it is only a temporary house designed for short-term living. Within our body is our soul, our dimension of personhood, of identity. Our soul is the important center of our mind, intellect, will, emotions, and all that combine to form personality.

There is also a third part of us — our spirit. This is our capacity to know and communicate with God. When things go wrong in the psyche (soul) or in the spirit, the clamor of inward conflicts attack the outer body in such a way as to get our attention to deal with the unseen issues and balances. Inward conflict is simply a *disagreement* between our body with its appetites and desires, and our soul with its feelings and thoughts about the activity and demands of our body, and our spirit. When these three interwoven dimensions of our being are not in agreement, harmony is disrupted, and we are engaged in internal civil war.

Interestingly, God gives an in-depth study in two short statements of the reason for *all* personal conflict. "For the whole energy of the lower nature is *set against*

18

the Spirit, while the whole power of the Spirit is *contrary to the lower nature. Here is the conflict,* and that is why you are not free to do what you want to do" (Gal. 5:17, PHILLIPS, italics mine).

It is this inner frustration and warfare that colors the way we feel about people, places, and happenings in our life far more than the happenings themselves. We can change the happenings many times, but we do not know *how to change our inner self.* The Bible goes on to give us the key in the next verse: "But if you follow the leading of the Spirit, you stand clear of the Law." There are several obvious applications to those words, but the one I want to consider is the fact that to "stand clear" indicates one who is free. God has laid out a beautiful plan for personal freedom for every person, and if we are not living it day by day it is simply because we have substituted our plan or that of some other person or organization for God's plan for our lives. *God's program works!* If our life isn't functioning in freedom and peace, then let's find out why and do something about it.

Jesus Christ is called the Prince of Peace, and when the Prince is in control there is peace. Any area of life that is in turmoil is evidence that God is not in control of that portion of our life — for He does not produce confusion or conflict. God has laid out a pattern for individual harmony as well as national peace, and it is quite a simple process.

The first priority is to establish which component of self is to have the controlling voice: Which is to be the final decision-maker? It is God's plan for the spirit to be always in command. The physical body, affected by every passing wind and the only short-term part of our being, is not intended to dictate terms to the two eternal parts of self. When the body controls the spirit, its appetites scream to be satisfied. The more food the stomach receives, the more it stretches to make room for its next increased demand. The physical body has absolutely no control over its demands, whether for food, alcohol, drugs, or sex; and it will ultimately destroy itself with excess if the inner person does not take intelligent control. The body is not designed with the capacity for leadership but is patterned to be a servant maintaining physical life for the more important treasures of soul and spirit that it houses. If total responsibility is placed on the body, it will break down, for that is not its function. A train must have proper controls, and an engineer must operate those controls if it is to stay on the track and reach its destination. Our total self is constructed to be under the operational management of our spirit in harmony with God, who is the directing Engineer, if we are to arrive at the station of peace and harmony.

The body is not the only anarchist that fights for control — the soul (or psyche) has its own set of appetites. If it is given free reign to control the total life, it will be somewhat like the crocodile who mistakenly swallowed a school of live piranha. Feelings can saturate the person with a self-destruct impact. Emotions were never meant to control the person but the person to control the emotions.

Feelings are a marvelous means of sharing the inner person with others. Tears melt hardness; the ripple of laughter lightens hearts and eases tension; a quick hug encourages a child; and when an unscheduled song escapes our lips like a bird in flight, it kisses our life with joy. But feelings are not reliable enough to be the guardian of our future or the determining factor for the present. The upsurge and downdraft of emotions change with the color of the sky. A gray day produces gray moods, and it is a known fact that more suicides take place on gloomy days than on sunny ones. The soul holds responsibility for many important functions, and it does not need the overload of having to carry those intended for the spirit, leaving the spirit with nothing to do.

It is interesting to recognize that the Bible does not contain one statement that tells us to trust God, pray, thank, or praise Him because we *feel* like it! There is no indication that God directs our life through feelings, yet we often bury tremendous potential behind the smoke screen of "not feeling like" doing a particular thing. Jesus did not *feel* like suffering the agony of the cross; just read what took place in Gethsemane shortly before the Crucifixion (Matt. 26:36-44). Yet He died there willingly, for He had mastered the secret of living life at its most successful best. His spirit controlled His feelings and the activities and attitudes of His body, and God the Father had constant access to that spirit. He faced the threatening mob that night in the power and peace of inward harmony. He was not torn by personal conflict that burns up time, energy, and resources, even life itself. To allow the body or the soul to control the spirit is like asking a four-star general to take orders from a buck private! It is madness.

The physical body is always reaching outside itself through the demands of appetites to find food and gratification for survival, the psyche reaches out for input from many sources, and the spirit also cries out for nourishment from a source that is greater than self. If our spirit seems to be the weakest area of our life, it is because it is suffering the malnutrition of neglect. Jesus gave us the answer to that need in John 6. His instruction there can be summarized in just three words, "Feed on Me." There was nothing cannibalistic in that gracious invitation; it is a passport to power. There is a sense in which all of us "feed" on each other. We are affected by those with whom we live, and our emotions actually feed those who are exposed to them. But how are we to "feed" on an unseen God?

Today I made homemade donuts and they were delicious! But I would never have known whether they were good or not if I had not chosen to pick one up and take a bite. When I did this, I received a part of that food to become part of my body chemistry.

Our emotional feedings are less obvious, for those appetites sneak up on us, and we often respond unconsciously through habit; yet definite choices are involved. I may feel a need for contact with something or someone and flip on TV or the stereo, read a book, or watch a movie. Those forms of input stimulate feelings, whether good or bad, for I have *chosen* to receive them into my inner self. I may also choose to turn from these external stimulants and pick up my Bible and receive into my mind the information needed to get acquainted more intimately with God. At times I choose to turn away from the constant access to food in order to focus my thoughts on Jesus Christ and His directions for my life. When I am lonely, I have the option of concentrating on my feelings or talking with Jesus, an activity we call prayer. When I *choose* to receive the input from God's instruction manual on living (the Bible), and to invest in conversation with Jesus, my *spirit is fed* and I am strengthened.

Either we choose to feed the control-center God has equipped to handle the demands of life, or we by-pass it and live with the stress of having short-circuited the power plant of supernatural resources. In any event it is our personal choice that is involved.

For almost twenty-five years I was totally unaware of the existence of this life-shaping fact. I thought of my life as being fate, destiny, a rat race, luck, chance, or a dozen other vagaries. Now I have reached the point of calling it like it is. The day-by-day happenings are not an illusive happenstance series of purposeless circumstances, but they are known in advance by God and are vitally affected by my responses or reactions. It is my personal answer to the happenings of my life that releases the power of God in my daily situations. And an integral part of the inner self is the temperament that identifies the uniqueness of selfhood.

Temperament is much like a filter. It receives inner thought from the soul, awareness from the spirit, and outer impressions from the body and automatically determines what to do about them. To laugh or cry, love or hate, trust or doubt, expect the worst or best, talk little or say much, act now or wait; when done without a second thought, it is the work of temperament.

The greatest communication problem in marriage, parent-child, and other people relationships is the lack of understanding and acceptance of the individuality of temperaments. It gives impetus to the often-frantic compulsion to "help" others think and behave as we ourselves do. It is easy to become confused, hurt, and offended when those we love or are involved with see the same happenings and yet react in totally different ways than we do. They do not laugh, sigh, love, jump, or speak as we do, and it is probable that they are not being intentionally difficult. They simply have a different temperament.

23

Jean Lush, a friend of mine who is a prominent marriage counselor, told me recently of a woman who had asked if her husband was capable of being a better husband. When assured that he was doing the best he could, the woman graciously accepted it as being enough and replied, "I just couldn't have taken it if he could do better and wasn't!" She recognized that he was not deliberately cheating her of that which she felt she had a right to expect, but rather that he was performing at his top capacity and that for each of them that capacity was different.

Understanding and accepting differences in each other opens the door to expanded living through exposure to a variety of viewpoints. Each person in his or her individuality provides coverage of a facet of life refreshingly new and different from ours. When temperaments are controlled and directed, there are higher levels of interest and learning among children, exciting activities, meaningful conversations, and love and harmony instead of boredom and frustration.

If ever a wife and mother has had an opportunity to prove this in the laboratory of daily living, I am that woman! Hal and I are as opposite as the North Pole and the equator. All who meet Hal love him at first sight, but they're not so sure about me. He excites the imagination and is a dynamo of motion, though seldom practical. He is the personification of the so-called sanguine temperament that I would like to term *the outsider*. A person with this temperament lives on the surface, always reaching *outside* of himself for pleasure and gratification. He has potential for a mile-high future that sometimes has trouble just getting off the ground. He races around corners or, more accurately, across country in eager anticipation of the opportunity that's just waiting for him to come by.

But . . . as his wife I see the same corner and cautiously slow down, wondering what problems we'll encounter that are as yet unseen. And that is only the merest beginning of our differences. I am as typically melancholy, with the *insider* temperament, as Hal is the *outsider*. He is like sunlight racing across ripples in a stream, while I am similar to the buried current that pushes the water along.

Hal, in times past, has been absolutely convinced he would make a million in a year marketing a variety of products ranging from processed french fries to cargo container units and floating docks for shipping. He has seen value in raising chinchillas and manufacturing food supplements produced from oysters, to say nothing of sealer coating for buildings that would never require paint. He has sold everything from transmission shop franchises to one-hundred-year-old Indian rugs!

And I have doubted them all . . . until proven!

Into this antithesis of the great American dream were born five physically beautiful children who were to supply the full-blown evidence that there are at least four basic temperament types and more than forty times four combinations of these basics. And our children seem to have them all! One is highly representative of the choleric or *go-getter* temperament with sound and determined thoughts and actions, while another is strongly phlegmatic — our *easy-does-it* humorous diplomat! (Thank God for this light touch of sunshine!)

If the casual observer visiting our home happened to be a man, he would probably feel a pang of sympathy and identification with Hal. He might even say, "Poor guy, how can he ever succeed?" But if that observer were a woman she would no doubt shudder at the insecurity for poor June and the children, to say nothing of the unfairness. However, if you were a member of the family, you would be most fortunate, for those very differences provide an inexhaustible opportunity to understand people in all stages and roles of life and to be enriched through daily contact with them.

But — in the problem years of our marriage we had not yet arrived at such a semi-mature conclusion. It just didn't start out that way. Most of our days were spent thinking, "What is wrong with *him* — or *her*?" Obviously neither of us felt at fault for the frictions that occurred ten times during a normal day and more often on the hectic ones.

The emotional warning bells had clamored a loud warning on our first meeting years before. That night there were over two hundred skaters at the roller rink, but only one dominated the scene — not just by his skating ability, but by a certain magnetic charisma aided by good grooming and an abundance of self-assurance. He seemed to feel he had the world by the tail and enjoyed giving it a healthy swing. I had felt a strong irritation at his cockiness and thought, "I would love to be married to that egotistical grandstander for just three days. . . . Would I ever change him!" We have been married thirty-four years, and I find *I* have changed greatly.

Who Do You Change . . . Yourself or Others?

Recently a young bride-to-be became confused at a wedding rehearsal as she was told how to walk, what to say, and what to do. Her mother, in an effort to simplify the many details, suggested that she concentrate on just three major things. She said, "Dear, think about the *aisle*, for you will walk slowly there. Think about the *altar*, where you will meet each other. And especially think about *him*, the one with whom you will share your life." The following night as the strains of the wedding march were heard, those seated closest to the aisle heard the lovely young bride whisper, "I'll alter him."

All too often as the rice is thrown and the well-wishers leave the wedding scene, one or both of the happy couple have already begun to plan the changes that need to be made in one another. It is our natural human instinct to attempt to change actions and attitudes of others when they challenge our own. *We* do not want to change, for it makes us vulnerable to possible hurt; therefore, *they* must change. And the fight is on!

We long for improved relationships without pain, and we strive to change others. But often our tools are in exact opposition to the longed-for results. One day I walked into a man's workshop and saw his neatly placed assortment of tools. As he worked, he would choose the right one for each job without even glancing up. He had used them so often on similar repairs that he had no need to consider which one would be most effective. And even if others could have done a better job, his response to habit was so automatic that no progressive thinking or action was allowed.

The constant daily exposure to one another in the family conditions each person, regardless of age, to expect certain reactions in any given situation. The tools of psychological defense and offense are then applied without any conscious thought. Only when attitudes, words, and actions are changed will there be a changed response in others. Then suddenly one is shaken from involuntary reaction and aroused to consider new action, for the situation is no longer predictable.

Today a neighbor brought me a plate of cookies fresh from her oven, fragrant as a Danish pastry shop. I was grateful for her caring kindness to me. Yesterday she seemed cold and unfriendly. Today through *her* actions, *my* attitude was changed. Suddenly I saw her as a warm, giving person. Similarly, when I change my actions and attitudes toward others, it opens the door to tender, gracious, or at least different, responses. If I am to change others, I must first change myself. But those changes do not come easily.

The Search for Identity and Internal Security

Today many people are lost in their struggling search for a clear identity. One day in a large department store I saw a lovely little girl suddenly dissolve into tears and trembling. Before I could reach her, the tears had become screams of hysteria. She was separated from her mother and did not know who she was or where she lived. A lost child suddenly confronted with the bigness of a strange world needs positive, clear identification. She needs to know how to get through the maze of strangers to reach her family where she is secure in love, where she is known and knows others. Tenderly a calm hand reaches down and takes her hand and leads her to those who care. She is still in the same store but no longer lost. The strangling fear is gone; her identity is restored. Once more she walks happily through the aisles of toys and childish delights. She is with someone to whom she relates and belongs. Every person has at some point experienced the emotional disorientation of lostness. From Eden to today man has clutched at passing broken straws as substitutes for the leading hand of God.

When our son Mark was ten months old and learning to walk, he found a hollow plastic tube, a broken piece of a peashooter, and hanging on to it desperately he turned loose of all other supports and took his first step alone. But a moment later his new independence was dealt a staggering blow as he discovered the empty tube could not sustain him and there he lay — a crumpled heap of pride and tousled curly hair, with feet that had not yet learned the skill of walking without help. External security factors are often hollow and short-lived, but the internal security developed through understanding of self reaches out to care for and understand others and enriches all life relationships.

It is this incredibly designed self that God has created and loves. He cares and knows when we feel we can't take any more. He tells us there is freedom in "Casting all your care upon him (Jesus); for he careth for you" (1 Peter 5:7). It is no longer we who carry our heavy load, for the Savior takes it upon Himself to carry it for us that we may stand tall and free — released of every burden.

Do you believe God *can* solve your problems? In all honesty, do you think He *will?* Our fragile human frames have the strange power to block the mighty flow of God's resources when we run *from* the problem rather than *to* the solution. By all means run if you feel like it . . . but run straight into the arms of God. He sees the total scope of your life from birth to death and beyond the grave to His ultimate purpose for you. Because of His foreknowledge there are no unexpected

29

crises or emergencies, only His provisions and purposes. When we focus upon the passing experience and our personal limited resources, we often fail to see the tremendous supply of wisdom and emotional and material resources available to us. We are like the child who saw only her lostness and was blind to the nearness of her mother.

Recently I read a newspaper account of a man who had spent thirty years hiding in a pig barn in Russia. He had deserted the armed forces of his country while fighting in Germany during World War II and sought refuge in the stench and dirt of the pig barn. For thirty years his only light filtered in through a tiny crack. He missed sunshine and rain, spring and fall, winter and summer in all their parade of glory. His skin had become a bluish white, and his eyes were permanently squinted from efforts to see the world through his tiny crack in the wall. Once a week a relative brought him survival food. When he finally came out of hiding, sick and desperate, he learned that he had been pardoned twenty-five years previously! He spent twenty-five wasted years of agony believing himself to be hunted and hated when he was neither.

How often I have seen life through a small rift in my self-centered point of view and missed tremendous years of success and freedom from all that limited me. But those years have slipped away, and I cannot change them. What I do now is far more important: my future begins new each day as tomorrow becomes today. Now, *this very minute*, is a brand-new segment of time that has never been before and will never return.

Today is the birthplace of the future, a time as unspoiled as that first day of creation; it has not yet been touched. It is a day for changing the focus of the past to the present, for there is not a problem that God and I can't handle together today! The whole scope of the incredible design of inner self is washed with the joyful freedom of a Savior who fills the God-zone, reveals self-identity, and gives life a purpose for a dynamic future that begins today.

The Why of
Self

WHAT a wonderful time to be alive! Through the use of Kirlian and other heat-sensoring photography it is possible to take a picture of a person sitting in a chair minutes after he has left the room! It is also possible to photograph physical and mental disorders long before there is any outward symptom of such a condition. But despite all the marvels of science and engineering, man has not been able to produce test-tube happiness in marriage relationships.

What happens to two people who in the marriage vows have agreed to become one and, then in life experience soon find that illusive harmony an impossible dream? Home is the reality center of living. It is the proving ground of our adaptability to change and our actual receptivity to the ideas and selfhood of others.

One major barrier to the friction-free relationship we long for is the unfinished emotional ties that have been carried over into marriage. Everyone has memories of happy and unhappy childhood experiences. When things go wrong or are less than we would like them to be, it is easy to use those memories as a comparison with our present situation.

Many people can identify with Tanya's experience. Tanya has had an extremely close relationship with her father. After marriage, she unconsciously demands that Ted, her husband, continue to fulfill the hero role. Comparisons become the order of the day; all that he says or does is measured against the unrealistic image of her father. As a result Ted seems to be lacking in many ways that she had not noticed before marriage. The characteristics emphasized by the romanticism of dating are discarded and replaced by the penetrating analysis of comparison with parents, home, and past experiences. Ted is not her father, and his personality assets are totally different. But to be different is not to be inferior.

Not everyone has Tanya's background. The extreme opposite in relationships can be equally true. Barbara has had an "absentee" father or one who has never satisfied her need for the protective, strong security figure. Instinctively she demands much emotionally and financially, for she is afraid her husband may also disappoint her.

The memory of a brutal father can trigger sexual frigidity or sudden feelings of alienation, hostility, resentment, or even revulsion for the husband. It is a psychological runaway. It is natural to attempt to protect oneself from hurt. To drop defenses is frightening but rewarding. It is the giving life that motivates others to give.

I cannot force others to value me, but when I value them I am often amazed to discover that they have a deep regard for me and have simply been unsure of how to express it. I cannot make others love me by imposing on them a false sense of guilt, but I can love them, and they will respond in their individual way. And, thus, my sense of self-worth is increased because I have given something of myself, and it is an investment in their lives. I cannot beg, threaten, or bribe my family into seeing life from my point of view or responding as I do, for they are not me. Their motivations, feelings, and attitudes are entirely different from mine or those of my parents.

Hal is not the man my father was; he is totally unique. I cannot expect him to do or be what my father would have done or been. Nor should I fear that he may do those things I disliked in my father. He must be free to be himself.

In a similar vein, I am not my husband's mother reincarnate. I do not cook, raise children, keep house, or sew as she did, for I am *me*, the woman whom my husband married.

A man must cut loose emotional dependence and expectations that his wife will do whatever his mother did. She is not his mother; she is a unique person. At the other end of the spectrum, he need not fear that she will criticize or reject him as his mother may have done, for, again she is a totally different person.

What an advantage when marriage is recognized

as a brand-new set of relationships rather than a re-creation of those of childhood days.

The highest authority for establishing happy personal relationships is God who created man. Jesus quotes the foundational law for marriage compatibility:

When You Marry You Sever

"For this cause shall a man (or woman) leave father and mother." The most important relationship in life prior to marriage is that of child and parent. Jesus states that at marriage this relationship is to be set aside and replaced by that relationship which requires oneness. It is not enough for a person to physically move out of the house in which he may have grown up; he must also move out *emotionally*.

Shortly after our marriage, Hal and I spent several months in the Big Thompson Canyon of Colorado. My mother- and father-in-law, who were very dear to me, were staying about a block from us. Frequently Hal would stop by their house and discuss plans with them before talking with me. Then he would tell me the decision they had made together as to what we would be doing in the future. Soon I found myself resenting the people whom I loved dearly, because Hal had not yet moved out emotionally from his father's house. He was as dependent upon his father for decisions as he had been as a child.

A husband and wife must be free to discuss and make decisions for the life they will live together. After discussion, if they both have a desire for the opinions of parents, they may choose to ask for them and gain insight from their experience, but they should never feel obligated to have parents influence the final decisions. Certainly love and respect for parents should continue after marriage, but not a dependency that is in conflict with the love a husband and wife have for each other.

Marriage is never an escape for parent-child conflicts but the beginning of an entirely new emotional structure. Dr. James Nelson, pastor of Trinity Baptist Church in Santa Barbara, California, said recently, "Marriage was never planned to *diminish* life but to *complete* it. It is two people who *combine themselves* to project a new personality on their community. What is lacking in one is supplied by the other," just as two halves make one whole.

Life is now shared by two people who are totally different in their combinations of temperaments, talents, and supernatural gifts as well as purposes for living. A part of that difference is reflected in their individual approaches to handling problems — approaches that stem from the value systems affected by temperaments.

Forgiveness Is Not Forgetting

Hal, typical of the outsider temperament, places little value on time; clocks, schedules, and calendars have little importance to him. But time is very precious to me. Before marriage we floated together on his enchanting timeless bubble where only the things that happened to the two of us rated top priority. Every bright, carefree minute was to be captured and each fragrant drop of delight drained into the treasury of memories. But after marriage I sizzled over his lack of promptness. I hated being late — even one small minute — and I especially hated waiting for anyone for any reason. Suddenly I was plunged into a post-graduate course on the fine art of waiting and fluctuating.

The same effervescent sparkle that drew friends to Hal before marriage, any time of the day or night, flowed on with or without my approval. His irresistible ability to have people of all ages respond to him assured him an attentive audience at all times. Colorful conversationalist, captivating storyteller, imaginative, exciting, he transformed dull happenings into fascinating stories. If events developed a bit of elasticity in the telling, it was never from the tinest bit of maliciousness or dishonesty, but simply from an inner exhilaration that moved him and others to new peaks of interest with each narration. The public lavatory was as apt to offer exciting adventure as a planned luncheon with the president of any major corporation.

But in the meantime his wife waited . . . alone. . . Unplanned delays that were inexcusable, late dinners when the six o'clock fires still burned at ten, and the suffering little wife was more seared than the meat. Birthdays and anniversaries were usually forgotten. Probably no one ever felt more genuinely sorry than Hal when those special occasions were overlooked. He would dash out and buy a hurried, wrong-size, kiss-and-make-up gift while I burned with the humiliation of being the forgotten wife. But probably before he ever got home with the gift he would become involved in a conversation with someone who was just too interesting to leave.

Even more devastating than his temporary lapse of memory was the fact that minutes later he could happily forget that it ever occurred. The past was over, and he had made his effort at reconciliation. Now he could return guilt-free to his enjoyment of the moment. If it wasn't with me, he would have found someone or something more interesting. However, I could not forget or forgive so easily. Coals of resentment fed by self-pity burned into bitterness, consuming physical and emotional energy. And the rift was widened.

Most people who have a strong strain of the outsider temperament find it easy to forgive and forget. Those who are strongly insiders do not; forgiveness has to be learned, and there is no such thing as forgetting. But God in His faithfulness will always give us opportunity to develop the beautiful character traits that are foundation stones in becoming a free person, and He does so through *exposure* to situations where there is a *need* to *use them*.

I have certainly had many phases of training in learning the singing heart of free forgiveness. And I am so glad that God does not demand that we forget hurts, but rather He tells us to *remember* them! In Isaiah 51:1 we read, "Look unto . . . the hole of the pit whence ye are digged," and many verses in Ezekiel and other areas point out that when we remember our past and our sin it is to highlight the kindness of God's love in having freely given full forgiveness. When we remember those things, we are to praise God that He has brought us through them and to thank Him for His love. This remembrance motivates us to forgive others in the same way that God has forgiven us. We need not waste energy worrying about the fact that we cannot forget, but should use every creative bit of memory in showing the gratitude we feel toward God for His investment in our lives. What a joyful interaction we have with the character of God when we are able to forgive others and thereby have an investment in their lives.

Forgiveness, the art of releasing hurts, does not come easily or naturally to most people. The computer of the mind seems to specialize in carrying a running balance of all accumulated grievances without attaching a price tag as to the cost in damages to one's future. I discovered that all the needling in the world could not persuade Hal to show greater love and consideration. That was the thing I really longed to have happen, and I simply did not know how to achieve it. I would learn that accusations and blame cannot trigger a response of love on the part of the person accused. Rather, they isolate us, for who wants to be with those who make us feel guilt and failure? I am sure my unconscious sense of justice shrieked that if I had been hurt, Hal should suffer also. He must not get off too lightly or quickly.

While the insider personality is busily stockpiling grievances as ammunition for future counterattacks, the outsider is moving on to new enjoyments. This is a major cause for increasing separateness in the lives of predominantly outsiders and insiders who link themselves together in marriage. The melancholy partner lives retrospectively in yesterday; if he thinks about the future at all, it is to worry that it will be a repeat of the past. The sanguine personality lives in the fleeting moment of now. Today is beautiful; tomorrow is too vague to be seriously concerned about it. And all things are subject to instant cancellation and change, including homes, furnishings, work, and friends.

Roses Are for Gathering

My rose-covered-cottage syndrome was mercilessly dissolved in those early years of marriage, but not without a struggle. I hated the changes that had become my way of life. My heart cried out, "Don't dare plant a rosebush; you will never see it bloom." But I failed to see those that had been planted for me. Some came in a corsage of golden talismans, late perhaps, but the kind I loved best. Others were long-stemmed red ones in a hospital room at the birth of a son. Sometimes they were wild roses beside a mountain stream where a husband dared share his restless spirit with me while the wind, rain, and sun sang to us together. At times the roses weren't roses at all — just plastic geraniums from a neighbor's windowbox that spoke wistfully of beauty and color where roses cannot grow.

A few years ago while I was speaking for a retreat in Canada, a lovely young woman shared with me the story of her roses. Her husband had suffered several phases of emotional and mental illness. Parents and friends had suggested divorce. She talked with her husband about their future, and he said, "I cannot give you a bed of roses, and I have never promised to do so." Later when she returned home, she went into the small rose garden he had planted for her two years previously. She cut a few lovely blooms and took them into her bedroom. Burying her face in their petals, she lay on her bed until suddenly she realized that the sweetest fragrance was from the broken ones. In spite of the thorns their fragrance filled her room. She said, "My husband has given me a bed of roses, replete with thorns and fragrance. Is a rose quite complete without both?"

I would have chosen my roses with fragrance only. A chief thorn in our home was our differing views on the use of money. Hal refused salaries, preferring the challenge of commissions. Each sale was an opportunity for a special little celebration, but my practicality shrieked in protest. Money was for paying bills, life insurance, and planning for retirement.

None of these held the slightest interest for Hal. Retirement was in the dim never-never land of tomorrow and might never come at all. He just couldn't be bothered with it. Money was to enjoy today. Maybe it was only a coke together, or maybe it was the purchase of a dozen hand-tailored shirts. "Why buy one? If it is nice enough to wear at all, buy a dozen and enjoy them twelve times as much!" House payments and groceries could be taken care of "tomorrow."

On one of those "tomorrows," Hal found a lovely green dress and asked me to try it on. Quickly I dusted off my sacrificial halo and said, "I can't afford it." But my real message was, "If you did not spend so much money on yourself, I would have more to spend on me. Poor me, I must do without."

Man has a foundational psychological and spiritual need to be able to give to the one with whom he shares his life. It is as basic as water to a fish. If a man cannot give to his wife and enjoy this area of fulfillment, he will begin sharing his life with someone or something else. A man gives himself sexually and materially to one who appreciates and welcomes him. To criticize the gift is to criticize the giver, and soon the giving stops. What joy is there in giving if it results in criticism?

One day when we were in a store, very spontaneously I asked Hal if he would buy a certain pair of shoes for me. I turned to see tears in his eyes and in amazement heard him say, "June Miller, I have waited for years for you to *ask* me to buy you something you really wanted!"

There are times in any woman's life when she feels the need to ask her husband for special little things, even as she asked her father when she was a little girl. There is still a bit of childlikeness buried deep within each of us.

There are moments when a man feels the need to assume the giving role toward his wife that a father does toward his child — not because of demands, but simply for the satisfaction of giving. A man who is told constantly that he cannot afford to do pleasant things for his wife can begin to feel he is an utter failure. Had I so conditioned Hal to potential rejection and the repeated suggestion of failure that he had begun giving gifts to himself rather than to me?

How often had we both suffered from the subtle suggestion of guilt and failure in an attempt to bring each other around to our particular point of view?

It is difficult to adjust opposing views on money, material possessions, and careers, for they represent a major security factor to many people and certainly to me. I could be counted on to lift the sacrificial voice of the insider, declaring loud and long that these things, as well as our actual home, should be wisely used and invested so that humanity (especially I myself) might benefit from personal efforts. Was it not our very lives that we were spending in the use of material things? But to Hal all these things were to serve the individual for his personal enjoyment. His carefree philosophy floated like a cloud of fantasy until at times it came in contact with the harsh, cold reality of everyday living.

I watched as he skillfully organized four radically different companies in one short year and sent them on their way to success. They ranged from sales and service of men's hairpieces to manufacture of wood carvings and totem poles! The thing that bothered me was that he *sent* them on the way to success! He refused to go on with them. His happy-go-lucky emphasis always stressed the word *go*. He dared to catch the crest of any passing wave of experience and thrill to its excitement as he rode it to see how far it would go. But long before it could reach the shoreline of fulfillment, he would abandon it for a higher more uncertain and challenging one. The final potential for lasting financial success always drifted away to be deposited to someone else's credit.

Like the restless breath of the wind racing on north, south, east, and west, my husband moved happily on to unexplored fields and the call of conquest. His classroom was the world of personal experience. Vibrant and eager to learn, his good retention made him an excellent student, but impatience prevented him from becoming a scholar. I would have willingly worked long and sacrificially to enable him to spend years pursuing educational interests in a formal college, but I refused to share his mobile self-training program.

Our perspectives on relationships with people were as different as our views on material values. To me, a friend is a friend forever. While I do not rush out to meet others, I have a deep love for people and an empathy with them in all their needs. I find it hard to turn loose of those whom I love. Perhaps it is just that I love long and Hal loves quickly, for his warm, outgoing nature draws people constantly. He loves them dearly, but those with whom he shares friendship today in San Francisco must give way to those whom he loves in Miami tomorrow. He doesn't lose interest in old friends, but new ones take precedence simply because they are with him. They are to be enjoyed here and now.

Hal feels the tears and laughter of others. I have watched as tears fill his eyes when a blind man crosses a street tugging on his seeing-eye dog. In his book *Tem-*

perament and the Christian Faith, Dr. Hallesby has accurately stated of the outsider, "He is never far from tears."* The shrill cry of an ambulance has become Hal's constant call to prayer as he whispers, "Dear God, don't let them be hurt badly."

Shall I ever be able to transform this bubbling, restless piece of humanity into a responsible, stable, steady husband? I hope not ever! It has been a mind-boggling, demanding adventure in expanded living that has stretched every fiber of our beings to learn to give ourselves, just as we are, to one another — and, equally as important, to accept those differences as the assets they truly are. Hal needs my stability and conservatism, the inspiration and creativity that are mine through temperament, talents, and supernatural gifts. I need the sunshine of his lighthearted, instant forgiveness and delight in little things, his flexibility to change. Like a magnetic net, the stretching process of opening our lives to each other has also opened our hearts and home to a great variety of people with all their different interests and activities. They have left their rich contribution of nationalities, culture, information, and friendship as a deposit in our lives.

A home begins as a small cohesive unit of two people who have committed themselves to each other to become one. As each discovers the how of self, this union stretches out over years, miles, people, places, and happenings to become incredibly rich, full, and free.

---

*Dr. O. H. Hallesby, *Temperament and the Christian Faith* (Minneapolis: Augsburg Publishing House, 1962).

45

The How of
Self

I AM willing to give my marriage exactly one more year if you will tell me *how* I can make a happy home out of such a miserable mess. But at this point I frankly do not see any hope," Kelly sighed.

We seldom "see" the whole picture in any area of life. Often it is what we do *not* see that is the solution to our needs. I am told that if you put a bumblebee into a glass jar without a lid, soon the bee will die, a prisoner of his glass house. What prevents him from flying up and out to freedom? Nothing! But he will continue to batter himself against the sides of the jar he *sees*, until exhausted by his own efforts he succumbs to failure and death. It is what he does *not see* that is his open door to freedom.

In the Garden of Eden Adam and Eve were free to eat of the fruit of the Tree of Life, but their attention was so riveted on the Tree of the Knowledge of Good and Evil that they did not see the open invitation to eat and live! God completes the story begun in Genesis in the last book of the Bible, Revelation. "To him who overcomes, I will give the right to eat from the tree of life, which is in the paradise of God" (Rev. 2:17). The tree ignored by man in the first garden stands preserved by God in the eternal garden for all to enjoy.

The things we fail to see and say can be important links in the chain of life relationships. A chief barrier to happiness is often that we focus so strongly on the negatives that failure is projected on the screen of our minds long before it has ever occurred. Why do we so easily visualize failure and loss instead of success and gain? To understand *why* we think, act, and feel as we do is the prelude to becoming a happy, liberated person. How that knowledge can be harnessed and put to work in practical reality in developing warm, successful, satisfying relationships is the purpose of this chapter.

The first step toward becoming a free person requires that you —

1. Relinquish Expectations of Self and Others

As long as a husband or wife, family member or friend is being measured against our own inner scale of requirements, disappointments are a guaranteed result. It is like trying to see the Grand Canyon through a keyhole. During the first years of my marriage I weighed all that Hal did or did not do or say against my goals, dreams, and requirements, and the scales were always out of balance.

I concentrated so exclusively on the missing ingredient that I had little time to see that which I possessed. If Hal was on time for dinner four nights a week, I concentrated on the three nights he was late. I took for granted the moments of harmony and let them fall at my feet unnoticed. If they had been emphasized and appreciated, they would have become the motivation to increase the times of pleasure for both of us. My perfectionist longings focused on that which was less than I felt I had a right to expect — a prompt husband, or at least one considerate enough to call. I looked at the sagging casserole and soggy salad and sarcastically emptied the bottle of dressing over the whole works. A little love and a dash of forgiveness would have revived the drooping food and provided an atmosphere in which to enjoy each other. Wasted efforts in food preparation wove a scratchy blanket of self-pity, and I wrapped myself well in it. My evening had not gone well at all, for it was not the way *I* planned it. I doubt that I ever cared whether his evening had been as he planned it! Thus, it did not take long to go from the "honey, you're late" to the "what, late again!" stage.

The English language is certainly a tonal language, for it is not what we say as much as the emphasis we place on each word and syllable that makes the difference. The glory of the morning sunrise hides its face as the teasing reminder "Someone left the cap off the toothpaste" turns into the thundering threat "So *you* left the cap off the toothpaste *again*."

Most people shrink from conflict, whether it is in the form of subtle hints that they have flubbed or in outright denunciations and accusations of guilt. The actual thing in question is often as irrelevant as a pair of socks left on the bedroom floor, but the attitude projected may initiate divorce proceedings. There is little encouragement to hurry home to the love nest that has been invaded by an angry hornet, male or female.

It is equally demoralizing to find that no one cares or has time to notice small daily accomplishments. Whether they are in the home, office, school, or factory, the little successes *are* the groundwork on which larger ones are built, and if the little ones go unnoticed, big ones may never occur. Plants starved for water do not produce beautiful blooms, and we water others with appreciation, gratitude, and mutual respect.

Why should Hal have the car washed for me if I never notice? Why should I see that all his shirts are laundered if they go unnoticed because his favorite socks missed the suds? Why should I? Why should he? Because neither of us is perfect and neither of us will *always* notice each other's kindness, nor are we keeping score of IOUs or ordinary marriage responsibility and consideration. But it is that special bonus of appreciation that encourages both of us to give of ourselves more freely. We do not give to get, but because we get we want to give all the more.

Looking each day for the one tiny good thing to add to happiness, even though it may be marooned in a sea of negatives, is the important habit that transforms hearts and homes. It becomes the lifesaver in stormy moments.

Typical of the insider temperament, I have always rated a high grade in the subject of cloud-searching. I can even find the hole in every proverbial silver lining. If I have $100 in the bank, I soon find a $200 need. It is not my nature to sing with excitement over the $100 I have, but to tumble into bleak despair over the $100 I do not have. Physically I may be rounding third, but emotionally I am still back at the plate striking out. It is simply not the norm for me to see how far I've come; I concentrate on how far I still must go. One of the nicest things about my husband is that he can be counted on to see the $100 we do have even if he never sees the $100 we do not have. We need each other in order to see the whole picture; he picks me up when I am down, and my vision occasionally takes over when his stops.

Even more important than the financial or material "have-nots" were the emotional ones. If Hal kissed me in the evening when he came home, I remembered he had not done so when he left in the morning. Why now and not then? Was this bribery? Was I suspicious? Absolutely not! I just wanted the whole thing all the time in everything. I wanted total perfection. If you asked me if I was possessively selfish or unrealistic in my expectations of others, I would have said an emphatic "No!" I felt I was being practical, logical, and unbiased and wanted everyone to be free to be themselves . . . as long as it did not interfere with my rights and plans.

I have never had a husband or wife in any first-time group therapy session tell me that they are selfish or domineering. Is it that all those who are never attend such a session? Or is it that we do not see our attitudes and actions as they affect others? When there are problems in family relationships, people tell me they feel lonely, abused, neglected, unloved, insecure, depressed and that they have little or no personal freedom. It is like an inventory sheet of the "have-nots" of life. But what of the "do-haves"? Do we take as much special notice of them? To be a "have-not" person is to put out the emotional welcome mat for the destructive effects of self-pity.

And that brings us to the second step of becoming a free person —

2. Turn Loose of All the Yesterdays

Some time ago a woman told me that she hated her house because it was much too small. Looking around my home she said, "You really have it made. Everything is so neat and orderly. Your furniture is new and clean. You don't have to live in the clutter in which I live." She went on to tell me that her dining room was piled with boxes and that her family could no longer eat there.

When asked what was in the boxes, she replied, "The children's old clothing" — clothes long since outgrown. Her home was so full of hoarded, unused, cast-off clothes and furniture that she had no room for new things. She felt she was suffocating in the squeezed-in lack of space. But any space would have eventually become as inadequate and cluttered. Other children could have benefited from the clothes her children could no longer use, but she refused to discard them for fear she could not replace them!

Those boxes represented security to her. Susie's dress had been bought in Oshkosh when she had known happier days; Tom's confirmation suit linked her to a time when her son was not involved in drugs and teen-age rebellion. But rebellion is not limited to teen-agers, and hanging on to all the clutter or the past, to all the "have-nots," breeds rebellion, the fruit of self-pity, at any age in life. One does not conquer by

52

leaning on negatives, but by standing tall in the freedom of release and by replacing old attitudes and actions with new positive ones. Joy surges into our life as we see the do-haves become building blocks in our exciting future.

From time to time everyone needs emotional, physical, and spiritual housecleaning. Cleaning out the demand closet of having others conform to our impression of what they should be, say, and do (even when we are absolutely sure we are right!) leads us to the next pile of debris: the good old days (that weren't all that good at the time they were happening) and the terrible failures of the past — not only failures of others, but failures of self mixed in among the broken dreams.

All failure in life is temporary. It is also for a specific purpose. I have discovered an incredible truth in 1 Peter 1:4-8 (PHILLIPS):

> You can now hope for a perfect inheritance beyond the reach of change and decay, "reserved" in Heaven for you. And in the meantime you are guarded by the power of God operating through your faith, till you enter fully into the salvation which is all ready for the dénouement of the last day. This means tremendous joy to you, I know, even though at present you are *temporarily* (italics mine) harassed by all kinds of trials and temptations. This is no accident — it happens to prove your faith, which is infinitely more valuable than gold, and gold, as you know, even though it is ultimately perishable, must be purified by fire. This proving of your faith is planned to result in praise and honour and glory in the day when Jesus Christ reveals himself.

God is entirely capable of saying exactly what He means, and He personally guarantees the validity of every word. He has said that your problems are *temporary* and *planned* to *accomplish* a valuable result in your life. The physical body will one day die, but the true person (soul and spirit) living within that outer shell will never die. The experiences of this short-term life in a human body are producing rich beauty and rewards for the eternal person who will be released to continue living after the body has been discarded.

These temporary problems, hurts, and failures, while not *sent* by God, will be *used* by God to refine and beautify life. Failure has always been an essential means of learning. History abundantly illustrates this fact in the lives of Abraham Lincoln and other great people of achievement. Lincoln was defeated in many attempts to gain office, and the presidency was one of the few elections he ever won! Before that time his business failed miserably and he suffered a breakdown in mental health, yet he continued on to capture the highest office in our land. Through failure and loss he gained strength, stamina, and wisdom to overcome tremendous odds. And today he is considered one of America's greatest presidents! No wonder he was able to set in motion the freeing of other men and women from slavery, for he himself had conquered the enslavement of defeat. When he ran for president, I wonder how many people said, "I just know he'll never make it. He's not the man for that big job!"

That which may seem impending failure may become ultimate phenomenal success. Lodovico Buonarroti held a political office in Italy for six months, just long enough to envision himself a very important man who must protect his reputation at all costs. Soon after that he denounced his thirteen-year-old son in a fiery rage for his interest in art, which Buonarroti did not feel an honorable career for such a family as his. But today the world honors the incredible achievements of that son — Michelangelo!

It is the years between our dream and the finished reality that give us trouble. As a young wife, especially with the added natural tendencies of my melancholy temperament, I found that I had nearly scuttled my marriage by constantly evaluating the flaws and shortcomings of my husband and others. Disappointment, defeat, and depression wait in the shadows of too much personal introspection and judgmental evaluation of others.

Today many wives come to me for counseling who are coping with the fact that their husbands have had an affair with someone else; they find it difficult to forgive and go on. Having an affair is morally, ethically, and spiritually wrong, but what is to be gained by failure to forgive? There must be a point of going on if the marriage is to recover — a going on from this new moment and experience, not from the happenings of a week, a month, or ten years ago. Many couples have found that this unwelcome hurt can become a learning experience — a time of taking a good look at where the marriage is, determining the missing ingredients, and learning to meet those needs to enrich the quality of the relationship. It can be the beginning of a deeper love and appreciation of forgiveness, or it can be the beginning of the end because of the hoarding of hurts. The past cannot be changed, but the future can be healthy and happy.

Some time ago a woman told me that her husband was unfit for business advancement because he had made a poor business judgment ten years before and it had cost his company a sizable sum of money. His company had kept him in their service and forgotten the poor decision, but his wife had not! Moral departures, intellectual imperfections, and personality problems offer golden opportunities to develop a forgiving spirit.

Humanity will always exist in a world of non-perfect people and culture; only heaven will be that ultimate utopian life, free of sin, fear, guilt, and flaws. But in the meantime, hearts and homes can experience a touch of heaven here and now as the sweet breath of gracious forgiveness and allowance for one another in a realistic way bathes past, present, and future in new dimensions of freedom.

Christ reflected that spirit when He sat in the magnificent gold-domed temple in Jerusalem. That day it was crowded with people waiting to catch His every word, when suddenly a scuffle broke into the calm of the teaching situation. The Jewish leaders dragged a woman to the front of the crowd and shouted that she had been caught in the actual act of adultery and under Hebrew law deserved to be stoned to death. Facing them quietly, Christ said, "If any one of you is without sin, let him begin stoning her" (John 8:7). Jesus simply suggested, "What about your own life? Are you free of that which you condemn in others?" The accusers slipped away. Turning to the woman, Jesus directed her to "Go now and leave your life of sin."

It is not *his* sins, faults, and failures or *her* sins, faults, and failures that one must correct, but *personal* attitudes and actions. In little things each day we find opportunities to extend healing love until it becomes the automatic expression of life. Certainly there will be deviations along the way, but the important gauge of progress tells us that our failures to be as loving, as giving as we would like to be are happening less and less often. It is a barometer that tells us we are moving toward greater personal freedom and strength. As long as there is life there will be change, for no form of life — plant, animal, or mineral — is totally free from change. Positive responses to people and circumstances help to insure that changes will lead to enrichment and happiness rather than to deterioration and decay.

The third step in the march to inward freedom is —

3. Accept Change in Yourself, Others, and Circumstances Without Feeling Threatened

One hundred million women in America are being bombarded daily by the voice of the liberation movement born from the seeds of political and social inequality. I am a woman, and I feel the pyramiding pressures of the news media and its daily analysis of the failures of world politics, national economy, energy programs, health products, and family life. My daily experiences amplify their conclusions. Each trip to the market adds to the shock waves of financial stress as I measure merchandise received against register receipts and checkbook.

The once-upon-a-time relaxing evening of television is now a mind-boggling, roaring, shaking illusion involving my entire physical and emotional reactions as cataclysmic disaster flashes across the screen. It portrays the annihilation of millions of people here in the area in which I live. While contemporary literature, music, art, and advertising tell me I must be free, they do not tell me what I am to be freed *from* or *how* it is to be accomplished!

I want solutions that work and that produce tangible results in my daily experience. Some presentations of submissive femininity make me feel I should be a wet noodle or a well-rung-out doormat. But there is nothing drab or colorless about having a dynamic God of all power direct and protect my every thought and action! I shall not be forced by fast-changing social trends to compete for status in areas in which I have little ability and no interest. Women who have been happy homemakers and successful wives are under no compulsion to join the ranks of the employed simply to become "liberated." Lack of training and employment background leaves hard-working, unskilled jobs as the only offering to many. Why should a woman leave her role as a dishwasher for thirty minutes a day in her home to become an employed dishwasher for eight hours a day for someone who cares nothing about her? Liberation that dominates and suffocates is far from liberation.

If I am to be free to be myself, it must be a self that God has designed and equipped with unique potential, and I must allow others to be free from conformity to my concepts. The winds of cultural shock are blowing strong.

A friend of mine who has an important role in international relationships said recently, "I am suddenly awakened to the reality that a woman's role in today's world is changing while I am baking cookies and attending PTA. But cookies and PTA are American institutions!" Shall I reject these or other institutions because they move slowly? Or are they an important opportunity to identify with others, to be heard individually within that group, to contribute to small waves that unite with other small waves to swell and form gigantic tidal fronts?

"I do not want to be swallowed up in nothingness nor do I want tolerant indulgence," today's woman cries. "I need to be valued for myself." Not a value that is simply a reflection of the efficiency of meals on time, laundry neatly folded, or family chauffeur service that punctually deposits the family members to their specific activities and as promptly picks them up again when they yell, "We won!" Nor is that value to be realized by being sexually available upon demand.

I know a deep joy in being Hal's wife and the mother of my children. I thrill to every baseball game in which Jeff has a part. I love Mark's music. I treasure the precious minutes spent with each of our children, especially my daughter. Those occasional days when Hal and I can spend the whole day together are very special. And deep down inside I also feel an individualism. I am a person with value entirely apart from identification with any other person or group. I am caught up in the magnetism of my husband's personality, and as his words and actions fall around me like sun rays I am affected by them. But I am not a reflection of them. I am myself.

Marriage or a career is not the destruction of individuality. But it can become so when anyone demands to be heard at the expense of silencing all other voices and opinions. When liberation is wrenched from another through opposing and frustrating their expression, it is not liberation at all. Personal freedom is rooted in the recognition of the value of others and their right to equal expression of selfhood.

All about us nature blends beauty without sacrificing individuality. The flaming reds and golds of sunset flow into shades of orange and pink; yet the red is still red and gold remains gold. Shades of color have combined to produce exquisite blends while still retaining distinctive individuality; and so it is with people. The recognition and sharing of values we find in each other opens the door to personal freedom and enriches all who walk that way. We are free to the extent that we free others.

Freedom is a two-way street. Current movements have focused attention on the fact that if women are to have the equal right to enter professions and sports that have long been considered as belonging to men, then men must also have the equal right to enter all fields of interest that have been previously restricted to women. If it is equality, it must free both men and women even though the cultural results pose new difficulties.

The principles of the liberated life go much deeper than the social, political, and economic considerations on which our nation and the world are focusing much of their attention. Jesus Christ headed the greatest liberation reform the world has ever known. He spelled out the bill of equal rights in blood.

In Galatians 3:28 we read, "There is neither Jew nor Greek, slave nor free, male nor female, for you are all one in Christ Jesus." This was written to those who are "children of God through faith in Christ Jesus." To these God declares a total equality as if racial, social, and sexual barriers never existed. When Jesus died on Calvary that sins might be forgiven and removed, it was for every person without exception. It is the individual acceptance or rejection of that forgiveness that determines family relationship to God as our Father. Through activated trust in Jesus, who supercedes all denominational lines, the Spirit of God draws us together into His family circle.

Having received the royal adoption into that intimate relationship, there is a new freedom of security; an ability to extend to others unconditional love and understanding. Tapping into the family inheritance of the very nature of God, His transplanted life in us relieves us of the compulsion to push others to become what we would like them to be. The Father loves them too, and they become His responsibility if change is in His purpose for their lives. In releasing others, we ourselves are first released. We have gained the benefit of our own giving! Resistance is torn down, and we catch a glimpse of others as they are: unique persons who never shall be a feedback or reflection of our personal inner dreams and goals for them.

Several years ago a mother longed to see her son serving God behind the pulpit of a church. She watched sadly as that boy turned instead to the world of science. But one day her heart leaped with joy, for suddenly she recognized that her son had a responsible part in carrying God's Word to the moon! What a pulpit God had chosen in answer to her prayers!

A rocket ship or a tractor seat, a bicycle or an elevator — if it is God's chosen "pulpit," it will be transformed because He shares it with His child. It is His presence that makes the difference. God must have the freedom to lead each member of His family in his or her development. And in the final analysis it will enrich the total unit and will not limit individuality, for it was His idea to create us as individuals.

Once life has begun, it cannot remain static. It must be open to change. Today social cultures, political philosophies, financial structures, and individuals are in a constant state of change. But before the first change of any form of life ever took place, God was watching and knew the end from the beginning. Revelation 1:8 states, " 'I am the Alpha and the Omega,' says the Lord God. 'who is, and who was, and who is to come, the Almighty.' " In Revelation 22:13, we find the same words. And Revelation 21:3-6 underscores this unshakable fact with this beautiful promise:

> And I heard a loud voice from the throne saying, "Now the dwelling of God is with men, and he will live with them. They will be his people, and God himself will be with them and be their God. He will wipe every tear from their eyes. There will be no more death or mourning or crying or pain, for the old order of things has passed away." He who was seated on the throne said, "I am making everything new!" Then he said, "Write this down, for these words are trustworthy and true." He said to me, "It is done. I am the Alpha and the Omega, the Beginning and the End. To him who is thirsty I will give to drink without cost from the spring of the water of life."

The God of Creation is the God who hovers over us through every changing moment and who guarantees the end result of our life if we are trusting in Jesus Christ. One day we shall look back on all of life's uncertainties and see them from His viewpoint. We shall revel in the life in which God has made all things new, fresh from His loving and yet mighty hand! But for today, we are secure in changing times knowing that God holds us and our circumstances and that nothing is new or surprising to Him. All things that touch life today have been known by Him since the beginning of time, and He has always been working in our life with the end result in full view. How marvelous to simply relax and turn from introspection, to look out and see the needs of others, and to move on to the fourth step in the journey to freedom.

4. Value Others and Be Excited by Their Discoveries and Accomplishments — Especially Husband and Children

Someone has said that cooperation would solve most problems: Freckles would make such a nice coat of tan if they would only get together! In my desire to be an individual as well as a part of the family unit, I want to contribute to an atmosphere in the home where each person has a healthy degree of respect and privacy but not isolation. Common courtesy in the home aided by a little cheerful thoughtfulness is an emotional commodity that nurtures healthy, happy growth.

As a busy wife and mother I do not have the time I would like to invest in many courses of study, but each person in my family has contact with interests and activites in which they are superior to me. Every person I have ever met can do at least one thing better than I, and I can do something better than many of them. I am not the musician my son is, but he is not the speaker and author that I am. My husband is a fantastic salesman, but I can bake a better cherry pie than he can. And so we gain from one another. Learning to explore and enjoy each person and his storehouse of information, talent, and experience, we ourselves become enriched. Giving for the joy of giving and developing a listening ear and an interested mind prepare us for the fifth and final step of this phase of our walk into freedom.

5. Be Pleased and Grateful When Things and People Work Out As You Would Like Them To, but Eagerly Expect God's Surprise Developments When They Do Not

The greatest dreams I dream are smaller than God's dreams for me. The most beautiful future I can imagine is greatly inferior to the one that is possible for me. I have a God who plans realistic challenges (not

63

impossibilities) that are underwritten by His guarantee to supply every need to succeed. But those designs are challenges that often point up personal limitations so I may see the end of myself as the beginning of God. The seeming vacuum is often the empty space needed for God to have room to pour out His mighty power and love. It takes rain clouds to bring showers of blessings. And it is the person who goes down into the darkness of the mine who brings out the silver and gold and riches of our Lord's design. My "mine shaft" was ten years long, but I have enjoyed twenty-four years of treasures since then, and there is much more to follow. It was worth it!

May our God sprinkle heaven's gold dust on your path today as you enjoy the refreshing variety of God's unique design.

Meeting the
Different Ones

Mother, if I invite Jesus into my heart, isn't He going to drown in the blood?" That was the simple logic of Jeff, our three-year-old son. A Sunday school teacher, unaware of the literalism of small children, would have been amazed if she had heard his interpretation of her lesson.

Jeff has been a constant source of refreshing good humor and unruffled common sense most of the fourteen years of his life. His happy, phlegmatic, or easy-does-it temperament carries him smoothly along regardless of what is happening or how excited or frantic the family, the town, or the whole wide world may be.

He seems to have been born with a missing ingredient — he has no panic button!

Pleasant things just seem to come his way in super-abundance, including good friends. He is tender, thoughtful, and has a warm sympathetic touch for anyone with a special need. But he would much rather encourage others to put out any major expenditure of physical energy to do things than become involved himself. He loves beauty in almost every form — from a sunset to a lovely table setting of fine china and crystal — yet he slugs a mighty home run with the baseball team. In most other forms of physical activity, however, he prefers to cheer others on rather than spend his energy in being too deeply involved.

He has a particular order, neatness, and efficiency in his room, with a place for everything except the dirty dishes that he seems unable to get back to the kitchen. His practical insight and analytical ability are often evidenced in business interests that seem beyond his years. The other day I went shopping with him for a waterbed, and it became a most interesting experience. I listened as he discussed the breakdown in cost of each part of the unit: headboard, liner, heater, pedestal, and small accessories — nothing was missed. Finally I asked why he was making such an exacting comparison. He said, "Well, it's your money, and I wouldn't want you to spend it for something that I would not spend my money for!" I appreciated his thoughtful logic. But he is not always appreciated by our other children who have more of the choleric or *go-getter* temperament.

Barry Goldwater, one-time presidential candidate, in making a guest appearance on a recent television program, said, "I am here tonight as living proof that not *every* American boy can become president!" That may be true, but if you happen to have a go-getter temperament you probably stand a better than average chance. Self-determination and will power seem to be the dominant factors in the choleric make-up.

Several years ago we were spending a summer in the Rocky Mountains of Colorado. I had hiked up the face of a mountain near the campsite with our small son. As the sun began sinking in the west, we started our descent. Several times I held out my hands to my stumbling child, but in stubborn determination he replied, "Me do it myself." And he did. The years that followed brought continual evidence of his desire for self-government: his own "do-it-myself" program for living.

It has been said by others that the go-getter can become the world's greatest leader or most infamous criminal, for he has a great potential for strong leadership. How important then that his values and goals be set in a positive direction. He pushes himself and others, and when the person with the physical drive of this temperament butts heads with the easy-going phlegmatic, the former is apt to get cut down by sarcastic comments from the latter. For the humor of the easy-does-it can become a defense mechanism against those who try to push him emotionally, physically, or spiritually. Stubbornness rises to the surface as ridicule becomes his counterattack to the physical aggressiveness of others.

The go-getter's emotions do not reflect the empathy of the outsider or the fluctuating joy and sadness of the insider; rather, he exhibits quick irritation at any opposition. Anger often spurs him on to greater accomplishments, as in the case of pushing through new laws, especially against wrong practices or false causes.

I have watched the play and influence of different temperaments in our home and the results that have added to our completeness as a family. If a busload of children should career off the road, Hal would summon aid, but he also would be the first to weep and pray. Tears would fill the eyes of our choleric son, too, but at the same time he would be rigging a stretcher or crusading against the lack of safety devices and traffic controls.

It is just too bad when anyone or anything gets in the way of the strongly choleric (go-getter) temperament — not because they do not care for others, but because they have one goal in mind and until that is accomplished they do not have time to be sidetracked by lesser causes or interests. A mother told me recently of her preschool son who has this temperament. His dad had sent him to his room as punishment for writing on the walls. Later when the father went to the child's room, he found him scribbling away on a piece of paper. Looking up at his dad with an angry scowl, he said, "Now I'm really mad, and I'm going to tell God on you! What's His zip code?" He was still "writing" out his frustration and anger.

Needing the Needling

What tremendous potential we have when we understand our children, even though none of them will ever be the total fulfillment of a general type, for we are all composites and blendings of temperaments. But when we welcome the variety in each person and help to develop valuable positive qualities, as well as applying useful purposes to reactions, our marriages and children can be transformed. Outsider Kathy who meets all strangers happily is not insider Jennie who drags her security blanket with her and refuses to talk. Jennie may not be a poorly adjusted child but simply a different temperament. Easy-does-it Tommy may have the family in stitches until go-getter Sam storms in involved in his latest project and kicks Tommy out of his chair.

When this happens, does the "parental guidance" defensively scream, "What makes you think you can get away with coming in here and starting a fight? Why can't you be like Tommy?" Cool it, dad and mom! Tommy may *need* Sam's push to get him involved and out of his somewhat lazy inertia. And Sam may benefit from Tommy's sarcastic needling! He may even realize that his project is not the only thing in the world and that he needs to show consideration for others who also have plans and interests. But as parents, hang in there; prayerfully love and positively guide each one to his highest individuality. Remember, you may be giving direction to two of the greatest men in the world of tomorrow! And God made no mistake when He put your family together. You need each other — just the way you are. And each one of you *needs* to experience the daily forgiveness of the others and the reality of the love and forgiveness of Jesus Christ.

Because we do not always understand the built-in motivations and drives, as well as the talents and gifts, of those with whom we share our lives, we often have expectations and demands that are radically opposed to the drives and talents of the individual. For instance, if I should ask my outsider husband to work away at illustrating a book for me, he would probably refuse. And I would be foolish to accuse him of not being interested in "my" work. But if I asked my semi-insider, artistic son to do the same thing, he would do a fabulous job and thoroughly enjoy it. I know that I can count on Jeff to happily visit an elderly couple and drop off cookies for them, but my go-getter son is much too busy. If the survival equipment for polar regions, on which he is working, is successful, it may one day save the life of his brother Jeff or others who travel in that climate. Neither is *better* than the other; they are simply *different*. And I should never expect the same response from one that I get from the other. They are not the same persons but uniquely individual as God has designed them to be.

If you as a parent have more than one child, you most certainly have several different strains of temperament in your children. It is a valuable asset to you, your home, and society as a whole. God will use you to develop these "different ones" and to prepare them for His purposes in life. Just think of the impact your life can have through the investment of working with God's children to help them identify and perfect God's treasured gifts. Certainly there is never a dull moment when there is so much variety to stimulate and to be developed.

There Are Two Sides to Competition

The most detrimental or even destructive tool in raising children is the competitive pitting of one child against the other, especially if the basic goal of the parent is for sameness in the children or in the marriage partner. If easy-does-it Tommy breezed through school hardly rufflling the academic or social structure of the home or school and go-getter Sam blows up half the lab, there is often the instant reaction: "Why can't he be like Tommy? Why do I have all these problems with him? I never lost a minute's sleep over Tommy." "Why does insider Jenny prefer to be alone most of the time? Why isn't she out with all the other children like outsider Kathy?"

We have been taught from earliest childhood that it is normal and healthy to play with others, and yet it is not the natural desire of all temperaments to "play with others" all the time. Certainly it is healthy and wholesome for any child to play with others, but the insider child has a natural capacity to *enjoy* creative activities and an appreciation of quiet beauty of little things that is best developed and enjoyed alone. The results of the alone experiences can then be shared with others to bring a new dimension of beauty to them. Sadly, many creative children are urged to constantly identify with the group so that their natural talents and gifts have little opportunity for development.

Drs. Jean and Veryl Rosenbaum, in their book *Conquering Loneliness,* have stated that a person who has the capacity to enjoy times of being alone "can be made to feel that being alone is strange, perhaps even bad." It is no more strange to enjoy being alone than it is strange to enjoy being with others.

Mental, emotional, and spiritual health is not packaged and dispensed to groups only. In fact, if the group is to enjoy beautifully balanced health in all of these areas, it is ultimately developed with the individual. There is a world of difference between escapism and isolationism of personality and the sheer enjoyment of being alone. It is not a component of loneliness. It is an elective, not a condition imposed by others over which the child has no control. It is positive, creative, and valuable preparation for future adult experiences.

71

The person who is fortunate enough to be happy when alone is probably an emotionally secure person who is not dependent upon others to a marked degree for security, identification, or even self-worth. In fact, his self-worth can be damaged if he is made to feel that he must be with the group to have value. In adult life there are many experiences in which we find ourselves alone. This can be an especially frightening time for the person who has had stress placed on group dependence and activity, for he is unprepared for such experiences. A child's play may well be the beginning of the development of supernatural gifts for fulfillment of God's ultimate plan and purpose for his life.

Each child is marvelously individual. It would certainly make life less complicated for parents if there were certain rules and guidelines that applied to every child. But the wide range of daily situations leads to constant enrichment and is a means of expanding our knowledge and personality. We do not grow by moving in the same circle of thoughts, words, and actions each day, but by confrontation that demands new thoughts and solutions. Sameness is easier but deadly dull and boring to child and parent.

We can expect our children to like different foods, clothes, colors, hobbies, sports, friends, and music, as well as having different responses and reactions to us, other people, and circumstances. They *are* different, and it is wrong to expect and demand that they be like anyone else.

Sameness is not the only goal of those who use competition in the home. Often it is an attempt to raise the quality of a child's behavioral or achievement level. If that competitive attitude is pitted against the achievement or character expression of another person, it will ultimately lead to feelings of uncertainty, failure, guilt, resentment, and hostility, even though the feelings may be disguised in bravado, swagger, or "I couldn't care less" attitudes.

If easy-does-it Tommy is not the achiever that go-getter Sam is, especially in projects and leadership, and he is expected to compete in a field that is not his strong point, he will probably make a poor showing and will determine that his parents or teachers are not pleased with him. This can affect him this way:

a) Because his parents or teachers are not pleased with him, he feels he has let them down. His worth as a person takes a serious drop; he is ashamed. The failure-guilt-fear-defeat-syndrome is set in motion.

b. When self-worth drops, the motivation to try weakens. Why run the risk of new defeat? If he did not succeed this time, he probably would not the next time, he reasons. The drop-out process has begun.

c. There is a strong feeling of alienation from his parents whom he has failed. But there is also a resentment of the fair-haired son of whom his parents approve and who makes him feel his failure most keenly. Sarcasm and belittling of his brother may be his reaction, or a sudden refusal to be involved in anything his brother is interested in doing. It may even promote the desire to break or steal personal things of his competitor. When his attitudes receive added criticism from parents and increased demands to achieve "like Sam," the problem becomes more severe. Cutting classes, experimentation with drugs, and a general indolence are often results.

But how does this affect go-getter Sam, "the winner"? His natural lack of consideration for others is fed to the point of possible cruelty or abuse. His ego disdains those who can't keep up with him. And he has little sympathy for the silly sentimentality of the outsider or insider. His rugged determination to finish what he starts adds fuel to the domineering contempt he feels for the pleasant, easy-going, humorous one who lacks his drive and fast-thinking practicality.

Encouraging a child to compete with his brother or sister implies a winner and a loser. But even the winner's prize has debatable value. It may breed temporary higher achievements in sports, learning, or other areas, but it tears down the value system of the person involved. It also makes future success and worthwhile use of supernatural gifts a remote possibility. Barriers are built between children, and barriers of mistrust are erected against parents and adults. The child who feels himself a loser feels betrayed by adults; he has been unfairly judged. Partiality seems to be the order of the day, and it becomes a divisive factor between parents and children.

Usually in the process parents themselves become divided against each other. Without realizing what has happened, mother may sense that dad is demanding too much and interprets it as favoritism of one child above another. Her sense of fair play may be outraged, and she attempts to compensate by giving the underdog unearned extra privileges, goodies, gifts, and even coddling. The father may recognize that she is showing sympathetic favoritism to one child and interpret it as defiance of his discipline or a lack of confidence in his

74

wisdom and love for the children. He may become aggressively demanding of her and the children (depending on his own particular temperament), or he may throw in the towel and relinquish leadership entirely.

The most well-informed ones in the home are the children who are keenly aware of the fact that mom and dad do not agree, and their world is threatened by the discord of those who should be their security. Sooner or later, they are forced into a compensatory favoritism or taking of sides with their parents. If Tommy agrees with mom that dad is unfair, he has let his father down and feels new disillusionment with himself. If Sam agrees with dad that women do not understand, he will probably push on harder than ever to bolster his position with his dad. He resents the unfairness of his mother and becomes isolated from her and his brother. Both parents have lost the wholesome respect and harmony that warm acceptance and understanding can produce and have greatly damaged their directive leadership and ability to successfully discipline and develop the children.

Every team must have a captain to avoid confusion on the part of the players. Every army must have the final authority of a general when battle strategy is laid out. And God has given that final deciding vote of authority to the father when there is a father in the home. When there is no father, the mother has the assurance of God aiding her in that administrative role. "Fear not; for thou shalt not be ashamed . . . for thy Maker is thine husband; the Lord of hosts is his name; and thy Redeemer the Holy One of Israel; The God of the whole earth shall he be called" (Isa. 54:4,5).

This same God promises complete forgiveness

and total cleansing from all sins, failures, guilts, and defeats as we bring them to Jesus Christ and leave them with Him. "For he (God) hath made him (Jesus Christ) to be sin for us, who knew no sin; that we might be made the righteousness of God in him" (2 Cor. 5:21). The moment we confess sin to Jesus Christ we are forgiven; the past ends in the birth of the future which takes place that very moment, and God Himself shares it with us. He promises, "And all thy children shall be taught of the Lord; and great shall be the peace of thy children" (Isa. 54:13).

As He teaches our children through us, we discover the only worthwhile competition for children in the home is a positive, happy competing against their own past performances. It should not be based on failure, guilt, or inadequacy, but rather on a recognition that the child is growing in mental, physical, and spiritual strength each day, each year. Therefore, there are new possibilities for accomplishment not achievable yesterday or last year.

Help the child set his own realistic goals for development within a reasonable time and determine what must be done to achieve those goals. To encourage and remind when he forgets or procrastinates is a valuable teaching opportunity. It is a time for developing reliability and the sense of accomplishment and increased self-worth that comes from achieving goals he himself can be proud of and respect. It ignites the dynamic will to do, the courage to tackle, and the confidence to follow through until the final moment of sweet victory. Parental approval, love, understanding and encouragement when they falter is an essential part of developing positive personal worth in the child who will one day be an adult.

How beautifully God underscores this important fact in all human relationships as He directs us to "Live together in harmony, live together in love, as though you had only one mind and one spirit between you. Never act from motives of rivalry or personal vanity, but in humility think more of each other than you do of yourselves. None of you should think only of his affairs, but should learn to see things from other people's point of view. Let Christ Jesus be your example as to what your attitude should be" (Phil. 2:2-5, PHILLIPS). Learning to see things from God's viewpoint extends far beyond our human family. It opens the door to our greater spiritual family and the treasury of gifts that are prepared and waiting for us to claim.

The Gift Shop
Is Open

WHAT an exciting day it has been! I have been searching every gift shop, bridal boutique, and china store in town for a gift for my daughter's wedding. I don't want just any gift for Joy. She's special to me; she's *my* daughter. I want something that will last her a lifetime . . . something she can enjoy every day . . . something that gets better with use and that will continue to enrich her life. But it must be practical enough to fit into the place where she and her future husband will live. It must be in harmony with their interests and life style, for soon the two of them will become one.

Today, as a parent, I understand a little more clearly how God has searched the holy gift shop of heaven to provide the best gift for each of His children. How carefully our Father designs our temperaments, talents, and gifts so they may flow in a complementary common direction for the fulfillment of the person in much the same way that body, soul, and spirit combine to become a complete person.

Like the rainbow of promise in a stormy sky, God has revealed through the apostle Paul that He gives gifts "to each man, just as he determines" (1 Cor. 12:11). Throughout earth's history, no person has ever been left out! In Psalm 68:18 it is said that there are "gifts for men; yea, for the rebellious also." This truth is reaffirmed in Ephesians 4:8. The rainbow touches earth and the pot of gold is nearer as we discover God has endowed *all* people with specific power to accomplish certain things.

It is God alone who determines each supernatural gift on the basis of His planned purpose for the life of each individual. He plans ahead, knowing where we will live, who we will marry (or not marry), and what work we will do. He knows the gift that has the capacity to produce joy each day and accrued happiness through the years. It is the provision for self-value and completeness. There can be no total fulfillment except through the use of these God-given gifts. When they are dormant and unrecognized, a person will suffer conflicts, frustration, and a degree of failure because the power plant has been turned off — or, more accurately, has never been turned on!

God knows a secret that no one else knows — He knows why we are here, why we were born to this particular set of parents, in this place, and at this exact moment in time. He has a reason for our being, a plan for our future, and He does not plan failures. Though we may pass through what seem to be failures, we do *pass through* them. These experiences then become tools in developing strength of character, wisdom, and beauty and have a part in preparing us for the ultimate success that is possible. The special provision for the accomplishment of it all is His love-gift.

God urges us to discover and use His gifts and His plans for liberated lives that have resources greater than any need. Those gifts and our natural temperaments are deeply interrelated. Contrary to popular opinion, I do not believe there is such a thing as basic weakness of temperament, nor can I find any scriptural basis for it. Such weakness implies that we are less than complete in original design.

God is the Design Engineer of our lives, and we do not need to be fearful of flaws in His design. In Genesis 1:27 we read, "God created man in his own image, in the image of God created he him; male and female created he them." At the end of the creation period He proclaimed that all He had made up to that point, including man and woman, was "very good." There is no basic weakness in the God who made man in His image, nor does the Bible speak of any such weakness.

But what of the flaws and inconsistencies in our lives? Certainly we are far from perfect, for sin has left its escalated impact on the physical as well as the moral structure of lives today. God has given mankind freedom of choice — freedom to choose to ignore God, at least for the time being. But there will be a final accounting for what we have done with God's designed person. God, at great expense — the life of His Son Jesus Christ — has overcome sin for each person who

81

chooses to receive and rely on that provision. Man also has the freedom to reject God's plan and purpose for self. The Bible calls such action sin, not weakness. We have inherited the nature of Adam, not the temperament. For temperament is highly personal and individual, and the responsibility for what we do with it is just as individual. It was not man's basic weakness, but the strength of the power of choice that got him into trouble in Eden, and it is the strength of choice that will lead him out of sin and on to glory.

Come Alive to Hidden Strength

The ability to make a choice and realize worthwhile, profitable results is a tremendous satisfaction and source of fulfillment. It is the impact of the individual upon his world; it is his capability to direct his affairs well and to affect others through his choices.

No one can trigger the responses and reactions of the people with whom you have contact the way you can. What you do with your life today will have an effect long after you are dead through the stamp of your words, actions, and attitudes on the memory and personality of others. Your influence does not end at the grave. Every choice makes an impact on someone and has the potential to generate dynamic power. It was the negative use of this strength and power that sent marriage reeling, shattered parent-child relationships, and evoked the uprooting of earth's first family unit. The precedent of guilt, fear, and rebellion was established. Strength unwisely used, not weakness, is to be credited with that change.

Man's greatest strength becomes his most dangerous enemy when it is withheld from God. When an individual rejects the loving wisdom of God's government and direction in any area of life, that part is short-circuited, at least temporarily, from the positive activity and plan of God.

Adam and Eve were created for fellowship with God, and that fellowship was violently ruptured when they refused to abide by His one protective stipulation that was intended to shield them from exposure to the devastating knowledge of evil.

Can you imagine life with only knowledge of good? How tremendous it would be to be able to walk in New York City's Central Park, or on any street, beach, or mountain, free of fear or even the threat of danger. To be bathed in the light of the moon and stars or warmed by the sun's rays without ever a thought of drought, storms, famines, disease, or war, to say nothing of the uprooting separation from those we love. It is not God's choices that are or were at fault. All traumatic conditions and confrontations of life were born in the abuse of man's strength, his freedom of choice, almost 6,000 years ago and are amplified by personal decisions now.

Developing Limited Strength Through Control of Self

Today, freedom of choice has escalated with the increase of people and the multiplied options available. We live in an incredibly wide world of alternative thoughts and actions. But comparative choices are not unique to today's culture. From beginning to end, the Bible is a comprehensive analysis of the decisions of man in dependence upon God and man apart from God — the difference of these decisions and their results. There are sharp contrasts in their approaches to handling problems and all life relationships. Those approaches may also reflect the impact of temperament. But it is an impact of strengths rightly or wrongly used rather than weakness.

Receiving Unlimited Strength from an Outside Source

In 2 Corinthians 12:9 we read, " 'My grace is enough for you: for where there is weakness, my power is shown the more completely.' Therefore, I have cheerfully made up my mind to be proud of my weaknesses, because they mean a deeper experience of the power of Christ" (PHILLIPS). The Greek word translated weakness is *asthenia*, meaning to be without strength. God assured Paul in this verse that when he did not have strength in any area of life, God had an abundance to pour into that very need. That's being on the front line for miracles! When any child of God is without strength, it's time to get excited! Relinquishment of emptiness and impotent self-control opens the vaults of heaven. If self has been like a dungeon of gloom, it can now become the treasury of God.

Recently I had the thrilling experience of visiting the ancient city of Petra in Jordan. Rising out of the barren desert, this gigantic mass of rose-red rock towers in stark magnificence hundreds of feet in the air. It dates back in antiquity thousands of years, touching the lives of many of the Old Testament characters. It was known in those days as Mount Seir and at one point in history had over 267,000 inhabitants in addition to great herds of livestock. The home of the Edomites and the ancestors of Herod Antipas and Herod the Great, it was still a magnificent city during the life of Christ.*

The only entrance into Petra is through solid rock

---

*Joseph Hoffman Cohn, *The Man From Petra* (American Board of Missions to the Jews, 1961).

walls towering over 300 feet high, and the passageway, called the Great Siq, is only about six feet wide in places. It is an incredible sight to go through the awesome splendor of the entrance and suddenly catch the first glimpse of its most impressive building, Il Khazneh or the Treasury. It, like all of the original buildings, is carved from the solid rock and leaves unanswerable questions as to how this magnificent construction was achieved thousands of years ago. The Treasury was never a traditional treasury, but rather was designed to be a massive tomb. Perhaps it was regarded as the Treasury because of the ancient custom of burying great wealth with the body of the dead person.

How typical of men to hoard priceless treasures in a tomb. What a senseless waste. But God would reverse the process. He would take us from life in the "tomb" to life in His treasury of incredible wealth. The passageway may be narrow, and certainly there is only one entrance into the life that God has made possible for every person. Jesus said, "I am the way — and the truth and the life. No one comes to the Father except through me" (John 14:6). Like the Great Siq, Jesus is the entrance into all that God has planned for you and me. If the pathway seems difficult, it is gloriously worth it, for you will find yourself rounding the bend and suddenly catching a breathless glimpse of His treasures for you. But if you do not take the first step, you will never know what God had planned for your happiness and success. It's there — waiting to be claimed. It's in Jesus.

Man builds tombs and God develops treasures; man thinks of weakness and God builds strengths. There was a time in the settling of the United States when the West seemed to be the weakest part of our country. It was undeveloped and there was lawlessness and conflict on every hand. But the West was far from weak. Eventually gold and oil were discovered and brought the people west in droves and sent the money east by the millions. Ever since then millions have become billions as the great agricultural and industrial growth of the West has fed the nation.

Undeveloped territory where the rule of law and order has not yet been established is far from weakness, whether in a nation or an individual life. Under the governing direction of God, temperaments expand natural strengths and possibilities for greater strengths become evident in implementing supernatural gifts. How marvelous to see that the very area of seeming weakness is the channel which God will effectively fill with Himself. Have you been cataloging your "weaknesses"? Throw away the crutch and walk, leap, run with the new joy of His greater strength!

In Psalm 84:7 we are told that by choice we move "from strength to strength." Each step up the ladder improves the view and provides the foundation for the next step.

All of us want to experience love, joy, peace, forgiveness, wisdom, and strength, and they are all resident in Jesus Christ. They have their origin in God. The life that is closely under the direction of God has the richest store of these characteristics in open stock, ready for instant use. Whatever area in life that is lacking or in conflict is simply an indication of the need to have Jesus fill it with the fullness of Himself. "For in Christ *all* the fullness of the Deity lives in bodily form, and *you have this fullness in Christ*" (Col. 2:9,10, italics mine). Jesus is the Completer of our lives, and until we permit Him to do so there will always be a zone

86

that is empty and unsatisfied. It is the God-zone of undeveloped territory.

The greater the emptiness of our lives, the more room there is for Jesus. The deeper our needs, the more abundant will be His supply, because He meets needs! As we welcome His entrance into our lives and throw open the door to each hidden recess, the warmth of His love and His mighty power are released within us so that He may reach out through us. In the exchange of our emptiness for His fullness, we move from natural to supernatural living!

From Natural to Supernatural Living

HOW can I discover my gifts, and how can I use them to transform my life and home?" In retreats and seminars around the world people are asking this question. I find that people of all ages have a deep desire to unlock their potential and to know more of life at its best. My friend Dr. Elly Beerman De Ross met me recently in Amsterdam, and we talked of the needs of women in her country who were ravaged by the Nazis during World War II. Their experiences are different from those of most of us here in America who have never known the devastation of war and starvation, but their basic needs are the same.

It is essential for all people everywhere to find a power greater than their own resources to whom they can turn in their emptiness and limitations. The power is Jesus Christ, and He operates through the particular gifts He has given each person.

Needs are the basis for miracles and are an invitation to have God perform His supernatural work in our lives. All miracles of God are given to meet some form of need. He does not pamper His children by doing for them that which He has equipped them to do for themselves, but He goes beyond their limitation with supernatural action and supply. His gifts to each person are a constant source of expansion of natural ability to supernatural results.

First Corinthians 2:14 draws an interesting comparison: "The man without the Spirit does not accept the things that come from the Spirit of God, for they are foolishness to him, and he cannot understand them, because they are spiritually discerned." The natural man (the man without the Spirit) is one who is dependent upon the nature with which he was born — his natural desires, ambitions, feelings, and thought patterns control and direct his life. But the spiritual man is one who has recognized to some degree his inability to resist sin and to effectively handle the problems and opportunities of life. Believing God's provision for the need is in Jesus Christ, he opens his life to welcome the forgiveness and leadership of God through the Holy Spirit. He is no longer limited to natural instincts and reason but has access to a greater dimension of God's resources, the supernatural life.

"The carnal man sees no further than carnal things. But the spiritual man is concerned with the things of the spirit. The former attitude means, bluntly, death: but the latter means life and inward peace. And this is only to be expected, for the carnal attitude is inevitably opposed to the purpose of God, and neither can nor will follow his Law. Men who hold this attitude cannot possibly please God. But you are not carnal but spiritual if the Spirit of God finds a home within you" (Romans 8:6-9, PHILLIPS).

Man's natural reaction to people and circumstances is often in direct opposition to the way God would have him respond. It is human nature to protect self and to fight back, attack, or accuse when feelings are hurt. But it is the spiritual nature that offers forgiveness and restores broken relationships. Natural instincts often isolate while spiritual love brings healing to others and freedom to the one who gives it.

It is this polarization between the natural and spiritual, between needs and God-given supply, that can be an indicator of God's special gifts to each person.

One day I made an amazing discovery. My needs had become increasingly heavy, and taking pen and paper I made a short inventory of major problem areas in my life. Typical of the insider, I found mine began with these three things:

1. Inability to cope with discouragement, defeat, and depression.

2. Negative or pessimistic outlook on circumstances.

3. Demanding, critical, and sarcastic attitudes toward others.

Then I listed what I was doing in an effort to correct these problems. My list of "solutions" ran something like this:

1. Sleeping in. Avoiding situations I feel I cannot

handle (including discipline of the children).

2. Urging (nagging would have been a better word) Hal to do more to ensure an acceptable security blanket. Hanging on to anything or anyone that looks like relief from insecurity.

3. Constant preoccupation with stronger ways to convince others how really wrong they are.

When I actually put it down as honestly as I knew how and saw it in black and white, it seemed utterly ridiculous that any thinking adult could be so foolish and illogical in attempting to cope with problems.

Would you like a bit of insight into your problems and solutions? Try the same little checkup and discover what is actually happening in your life.

After that I asked myself what I felt would be the best solution for all three areas of inner and outer conflict. It was obvious that I needed to do exactly the opposite of what I had been doing. I needed to:

1. Face the issues and find a basis of encouragement for myself.

2. Find a reason to hope in spite of temporary difficulty and look for the first glimmer of positive results.

3. Thank, appreciate, and encourage others.

Those three simple steps sounded very easy . . . on paper. But I found it was to be a rebuilding process that would last a lifetime. It has produced such beautiful results that I still find it hard to believe that my life has become so thrilling and rewarding. Since that beginning over twenty years ago I cannot remember ever experiencing the overwhelming discouragement, defeat, and depression that was once my daily life.

During the initial stages of changing patterns I found a treasure I did not know I had, and it has been of inestimable value. *I found my special gift.* In Romans 12 and 1 Corinthians 12 God's special gifts are listed. One of them is the gift of encouragement, and this lovely gift was my special endowment.

As I began discovering that God had a gift for me, I began asking Him to help me gain the most from it. One day I read Isaiah 50:4: "The Lord God hath given me the tongue of the learned, that I should know how to speak a word in season to him that is weary." I realized that my gift was His chosen channel for the release of His Spirit of encouragement through me to others. When it was in operation, *my greatest need* would be met abundantly and I would know the unquestionable reality of a God who was exceedingly able to meet life's deepest needs.

With the gift, He has given natural talents, particularly those of being able to speak and write, that the gift might be shared and communicated to others. How beautifully our lives are woven together with such intricate design to produce the tapestry of fulfillment and inner freedom. It is the caring, careful planning of God that reserves empty channels in our temperament so He may flood them with the supernatural strength of Himself. Like veins of gold shining in the hidden recesses of the rocks, He plants His treasures in each life.

I have shuddered to think of the results if my gift had remained lost in the closet of excusing my "weaknesses" as "just being the way I am." This provision for my needs would have been wasted, and all the psychologists, medical doctors, and spiritual advisors in the world could not have done for me what Christ has done through the development of God's gift.

Is the gift of encouragement the gift God gives to all people who have a major strain of the insider temperament? Not at all. The Bible mentions three groups of gifts for three different purposes, and God gives to the individual that which will best enable him to accomplish His purpose for being. As there is matchless harmony of purpose and design in nature and all of creation, there is even greater perfection in the interweaving of temperament, talents, and gifts in the individual's life.

Communication Takes More Than One

Each temperament type has its own special form of communication. The insider often leaves the impact of his thoughts upon the world in fine art and philosophy, but the outsider uses direct, instant communication through words. Both have unique value in meeting the needs of others, and neither is quite complete without the other.

Recently while in Rome I visited the Vatican. I was overwhelmed with the magnificent art of insider Michelangelo. But it was my outsider guide whose words and bright enthusiasm explained the philosophy behind many of the works of art and made the fuller communication possible. I was enriched by the skillful use of both temperaments.

The world receives much from the ability God has given the insider in music, art, writing, sculpture, theoretical sciences, philosophy, medicine, and many other fields. Theirs is a temperament that can actually enjoy self-sacrifice, and it takes that kind of discipline to develop quality in the fine arts and other areas in which they excel. To accentuate their talents they have fine analytical minds and emotional responses to feel the pain and joy of others so their art or work may reflect reality. Coupled with this there is often the desire to be still and meditate.

It is easy, though, for insiders to fall into the vacuum between ideals and performance, for it is difficult for them to move out of their thought-world to translate philosophy into life experience. Like the rainbow of promise, the gift of encouragement draws them out of self to new freedom. It is only when the person inverts the abilities of evaluation and meditation and continually dissects himself and others that the world narrows down and the sky seems to fall. But there is a God behind the sky, and He would draw us to look up into His face and turn aside from the view of self to see Him as He is and to share that vision with others.

It is the *failure to fill* the power source of the mind with valuable information and inspiration and to use it for positive purposes that leaves us susceptible to guilt and defeat, regardless of temperament. Neglect and misuse deteriorates the tremendous God-given resources of the mind. The greater the potential, the greater may be the void or negative influence if it is abused or ignored. The capacity is there whether we choose to use it positively or negatively, and the results affecting our life as well as others will be evidenced in great strength or great need.

By contrast, the outsider or sanguine man or woman may easily open the door of interest and understanding for others, but it is difficult for him to recognize God's special gifts to him. He, like all other temperaments, may find them most quickly by determining the area of greatest need or conflict in his life. Very probably he will find his gift is the exact opposite of that particular problem.

For many years Hal and I had constant problems with financial matters. He felt the chief use of money was to give pleasure to himself. And then one day he discovered that just the reverse was true. The top priority for the use of money became the privilege of using it to meet the needs of others, for God had given him the gift of giving. It is easy to focus attention on self instead of God or others in any area of life, but especially in finances. Money represents security and the means for doing things we want to do. It is contrary to human nature to think of giving away either security or something we actually want. Yet money offers little security: its value changes; it can be lost or taken away in a matter of seconds, especially in a major emergency. God alone is our security, and He is quite capable of handling our present and future "emergencies."

Psalm 37:4 became Hal's theme song: "Delight thyself also *in the Lord;* and he shall *give* thee the desires of thine heart" (italics mine). What does a person get out of giving besides an empty pocket? God has opened the storehouse of heaven to pour material and spiritual wealth into our hearts and our home, for God will never be any man's debtor. We can never begin to give more than He has given us. Our most is such a small token return of His giving to us. He has provided this fantastic world for our home and gave us five wonderful children. He has given me health after cancer, and He has packed every inch of our home with His love, peace, joy, and presence, to say nothing of His future provisions for us in the ageless expanse of eternity. He even gave His only Son Jesus that we might enjoy marvelous friendship with Himself. How could we ever match that kind of giving?

The very areas of our life that we once attempted to control when brought under the direction of God Himself have been utterly transformed. Our greatest frustrations when filled with His gifts have become our richest source of fulfillment.

God often gives the outsider the gift of mercy. To show mercy assumes need on the part of one who is to receive it as well as an adequate resource on the part of the one who is to meet that need. God, through this open-handed person, has an abundance of resources.

By giving and showing mercy the outsider finds himself freed of selfishness, and the deeper giving of self finds its birth. His natural capacity for joy is overflowing, and he experiences deeper longings to share with others more of his time and his innermost self. It becomes the motivation to discipline his use of time and to become prompt and considerate. His work takes on new meaning, and unfinished projects are completed more frequently. Business concepts are followed through; all the bright potential of imagination and communication pours into channels of happy fulfillment. A deeper honesty appears.

The open fountain of emotions so alert and alive to every stimulation finds the transforming touch of feeling God's love and sharing it with others. Certainly he who waters others is first watered himself, for God does not let us thirst in any area of life and then expect us to broadcast to the world that He is sufficient in that area. Rather, He pours Himself into our need so that we know our God is alive and able. It doesn't happen all at once, but it begins when we take the first step of response to God. As we give a little of ourselves, He replaces it with Himself. If we want to grow quickly, we simply need to release ourselves into God's hands more fully . . . to take our hands off and allow God to put His hands on each area of our life.

The Go-Power of God

God does not require us to do any more than He enables us to do. He is a most reasonable God. He makes special provision for the successful function of every gift. He gives natural ability in appropriate fields and professions.

The easy-does-it individual may find his spiritual gifts in ministering to the needs of others, in helps, in showing mercy and love, in hospitality and teaching.

The self-confident, ambitious drive of the go-getter offers tremendous potential in fields of management, leadership, politics, and production. The keen mind, strength of resolve, and innate ability to make quick instinctive decisions are valuable assets when directed in positive, productive interests, but especially when under the direction of the God who gave them.

God does not simply endow us with gifts and potential and then watch from some remote realm to see what we will do with them. He is ready and waiting for our response to permit Him to enter our body through His Holy Spirit so we may actually become the expression of Himself in the world today. It is the sufficiency of His supply that is at stake, and He guarantees more than enough for us and others through us. "And my God will meet all your needs according to his glorious riches in Christ Jesus" (Phil. 4:19).

It is in the little Book of Philippians that we also find a clue to a second means of discovering our particular gift. "For it is God who works in you to will to do what pleases him" (Phil. 2:13). To every person who honors Jesus Christ as Savior and Lord, God gives an inward desire and enjoyment in doing certain things. Those things will always be in perfect harmony with God's Word, for He never leads any individual into actions or attitudes that are contrary to His teachings and commands. He does not command a person to do anything that contradicts His teachings in the Bible.

"It is God who works in you to will" — that is, to *want* to do specific positive things that are for His ultimate glory. He is the same God who enables you to *do* those things. The continuing desire, the ability to perform, and the joy that results are indicators that can point the way to the gift God has given.

There is a third possible way of discovering your gift, but it is by no means foolproof. It is through the objective observation of other people. Often others can see more clearly the special endowments God has given. But they may also see only natural talents or self-developed abilities that have little relationship to the supernatural gift.

Years ago, well-meaning friends assured me that God had given me the gift of administration, for I had training in that field and worked easily and well in that capacity. Those who told me usually had a need for administrative assistance and their view was far from objective. Others assured me that my gift was teaching. God has used teaching to enable me to fulfill the role and enjoy the gift He has given, but it is not teaching for the sake of teaching. Some have suggested it was the gift of hospitality, but again, our open door has been a means God has used of encouraging others who had needs. As we hear the opinion of well-meaning friends who feel they see clearly God's gifts and purpose for our life, let us be sure we listen most carefully to God and weigh their suggestions against His Word.

There is no such thing as a totally outsider, insider, go-getter, or easy-does-it temperament. There are predominate strains in most of our lives, but there are also many subtle shades of the other temperaments. And there is the continual transforming work of the Spirit of God that produces change in each one. There is no such thing as God pouring four molds and processing every life that enters this world through one of those four basic patterns. He has not done it in any of His incredibly varied creation, and He certainly has not done it with man, His highest creation. He does not give pat answers to problems or assembly-line distribution of talents and gifts. But He does create harmony among predominant temperament strains, natural talents, and supernatural gifts that is in perfect accord with His plan and purpose for the life of that totally unique person.

Someday Niagara may run dry; someday the sun may lose its heat; someday the ocean floor may be a dry basin of antiquity; but the God who designed them and us will never find His resources exhausted. The God of all mercy and giving is the God of all power and encouragement, and He loves you today and has gifts reserved for your fulfillment and happiness. Have you opened your life to the floodgates of His giving?

"Every good and perfect gift is from above" (James 1:17). "If God is for us, who can be against us? He who did not spare his own Son, but gave him up for us all — how will he not also, along with him, graciously give us all things?" (Rom. 8:31,32). For God so loved you that

He gave Jesus *for* you and *to* you so you might experience the joy of heaven in your heart until the day your heart is at home in heaven with Him. Give Him the place He has reserved for Himself in your life and enjoy each day as you share the Giver and His gifts.

The gift shop is open, and we need not be window-shoppers. Go in, browse around a bit, and you will find your gift, uniquely designed, ready and waiting . . . just for you.

How to Get
the Spectacular
Gifts

ANYONE can count the seeds
in an apple, but who can count the apples in a seed?
Who can take a tiny brown seed and determine its
potential to produce a tree that can bear fruit year after
year? Nor does it end there. That fruit in turn can
produce trees that produce fruit, and the endless cycle
of productivity continues.

Some time ago I flew to Luxor, Egypt, where I
visited the tomb of King Tutankhamen (King Tut). I
was told that when the tomb was first opened earlier in
this century, grain was taken from it that had been
placed there when the tomb was sealed over 3,000 years

ago. This grain was planted, and to the amazement of those involved in the experiment it germinated and grew! It is unbelievable that grain could have lain dormant so long and still retained the vitality to grow and produce new life. But all that potential lay buried in the darkness of a tomb for thousands of years.

Who can count the potential apples in a seed or the harvest from a single grain of wheat? God can and does! He tells us he has even numbered the hairs of our head, which seem to offer little potential. How much more carefully, then, He has planted the seeds of supernatural gifts in every life for happy productivity. But all too often they are entombed in the darkness of ignorance and neglect. We simply do not know they exist.

During recent years the floodlight of public interest has been turned on two of the supernatural gifts in particular. They are the gift of healing and the gift of tongues. In our emotionally jaded, reality-hungry society there is an ever-increasing need to relate to supernatural power, to find an experience that moves beyond man's fear of the future and failure of the past and yet has expression and involvement for the here and now of daily living. The gift of healing and the gift of tongues afford potential for the evidence of God at work among men in a way that is appealing to many people. But evaluation of the use of any spiritual gift of God should be considered from these three perspectives:

1.) Why has God given this particular gift?

We cannot determine the motives of God from the opinions of men, groups, or denominations. The Designer of the supernatural gifts and the people who were to receive them has revealed much of His purpose and direction for the use of them in 1 Corinthians. In fact, chapters twelve through fourteen are committed exclusively to this subject. The Apostle Paul, under the direction of the Spirit of God, wrote to the young church at Corinth primarily to correct misuse and misunderstandings of these gifts.

In the first part of the letter Paul deals with the believers' attitudes toward marriage, lawsuits, and innumerable other practical issues; then he opens chapter twelve with this comment:

> I want to give you some further information in spiritual matters. . . . Men have different gifts, but it is the same Spirit who gives them. There are different ways of serving God, but it is the same Lord who is served. God works through *different men* in *different ways*, but it is the same God who achieves his purposes through them all. The Spirit openly makes his gift to each man, so that he may use it to the *common good*. One man's gift by the Spirit is to speak with wisdom, another's to speak with knowledge. The same Spirit gives to another man faith, to another the ability to heal, to another the use of spiritual powers. The same Spirit gives to another man the gift of preaching the word of God, to another the ability to discriminate in spiritual matters, to another speech in different tongues and to yet another the power to interpret the tongues. Behind all these gifts is the operation of the same Spirit, who distributes to *each* individual man, as *he* wills (12:1,4-11, PHILLIPS, italics mine).

a) God states explicitly that He does not give the same gifts to every man.
b) All gifts are given that they may be used for the common good.
c) All spiritual gifts are given by the Holy Spirit according to the choice of God and God alone.

How thoughtful of God to underscore the fact that He does not give any one gift to all persons. Not all people have the gift of wisdom, discernment, healing, or tongues or any other gifts. Therefore, no one at any time has the right to criticize other individuals because they do or do not have a particular gift. Such criticism would be directed at God and the decision He has made since He alone determines the gifts He will give to each person. People are freed from the temptation to urge upon others gifts which they may possess, for only the Spirit of God can impart that gift, and it is not done by the suggestion or striving of any individual.

God respects the individuality of each person whom He has designed, and His wisdom is adequate in choosing the gift that is essential for each to realize his highest fulfillment — mentally, physically, and spiritually. How marvelous that I do not have to choose the gifts I think might complete my life, for my choices would be colored by natural environment, family relationships, and especially my limited ability to understand the past, present, and future. Like Paul, I find, "At present we are men looking at puzzling reflections in a mirror. The time will come when we shall see reality whole and face to face! At present all I know is a little fraction of the truth, but the time will come when I shall know it as fully as God has known me!" (1 Cor. 3:12, PHILLIPS).

Several years ago following the birth of a son I became very ill and had a temperature soaring to 105º. I simply asked God to heal me so that I could take care of my child. The doctor came in to check my temperature minutes later and found that it was absolutely normal and I was feeling wonderful! God had instantly, miraculously healed me before any medication had been given. Soon after that, I met several people suffering from various illnesses. I asked God to give me the gift of healing so that I might be able to give them the same marvelous release from pain that I had known. But God did not give me the gift of healing.

Instead, God has given me the gift of encouragement, for He knows that much of physical and emotional illness is caused by factors which encouragement can best help. Instantaneous healing can solve a physical problem at the moment, but the attitudes that may have contributed to that condition can remain to create new outbreaks. Perhaps the healing ministry that God in His wisdom has entrusted to me is the less spectacular one of consistent building of concepts that aid good health. I will certainly have less opportunity to experience the highs of ego that might plague me if I should be able to do a more flamboyant work.

Since that time I have often needed physical healing, as in the case of breast cancer. But God did not give me healing without surgery and the process of a radical mastectomy. There are times when God heals instantly without the aid of medication or human instrument; other times He heals through surgery and treatment by physicians. But it is always He who chooses the method that accomplishes the needed results.

God is omnipotent and sovereign. He has the power to do anything we could ever dream up, but He also has the loving wisdom to know when to say no! Because of His marvelous care for us, He chooses the gifts that fulfill His purpose in our lives. If the balloon of pride should begin to inflate, He has a good supply of pins with which to deflate us enough so that we may continue to be His usable delight.

It is interesting to note that in 1 Corinthians 12 the gift of healing is mentioned three times, and in each instance it is plural — gifts. It is the only one of the gifts referred to in that way. I suggest that it is in the plural because of our need for a threefold healing in our lives: physical, mental or emotional, and spiritual. Spiritual healing has eternal benefits, while the benefits of physical healing end with the death of the body. Mental or emotional healing often aids both physical and spiritual health for it enables a person to make the best possible use of his total self, and the results of that use continue throughout eternity.

Thank God, I can actively trust His choice of gifts for me and His choice for other people. It is His option to do as He pleases, for He alone is God! And He has said that He chooses to give gifts for the "common good of all." In the next chapter the completed picture of that truth is revealed as we discuss God's incredible plan for the common good — the abundant, liberated life of every child of His family.

The second guideline in considering the use of spiritual gifts is to determine the answer to this question:

2. What does God want to accomplish through the use of this gift?

Once more, any valid answer must come from God, not man. It is good to remember that 1 Corinthians 12:1 tells us the purpose of the chapters on gifts: "I would not want you to be ignorant." God wants us to *know* what our gifts are and how to enjoy the results of them in family relationships. He also wants us to know the complete work of His Spirit in our lives.

There is a forgotten four-letter word that, when applied, will allow the ripening of the full crop of the fruit of the Spirit. It is the word *obey*. God's commands are never optional. He simply says there are certain things we are to do and certain things we are not to do, and depending upon obedience or disobedience certain things will result. Many areas of life are optional, but not the specific commands of God.

Obedience is much like the flood-control gates of a dam. When we live in obedience to God's commands, which are designed for our success and happiness, the floodgates are opened. Peace, joy, and the entire cluster of the fruit of the Spirit flourishes in our life. There is no inward frustration or conflict; we are in harmony with God, and it reflects in our relationship with others. It is not that we earn joy by piling up so many credit points. But there is a release of joy when we are aware that God's principles are wholesome and right for our life and that we willingly want Him to have supreme control over circumstances, people, and places comprising our daily situation. It is an abandonment of self for the richer freedom of moving in the circle of God's glorious love and liberty. There is no freedom without law; there is only lawlessness. And the law of God for our lives is essentially one of liberty. "Through Christ Jesus the law of the Spirit of life set me free from the law of sin and death" (Rom. 8:2).

One of the persistent temptations to sin is the temptation to judge others who may be different in their life style or expression of self. This is especially true in spiritual worship. We must remember that no person or group has an edge on the truth of God's Word. God is the sole Judge. His watchword to us is that

> God works through different men in different ways. . . .
> God has arranged all the parts in the one body according to his design. . . . that the body should work together as a whole with all the members in sympathe-

tic relationship with one another. . . . you are *together* the body of Christ (1 Cor. 12:6,18,25,27, PHILLIPS, italics mine).

God uses visible material and physical realities to picture invisible spiritual and eternal truths so we may understand them. The human body is a picture of the spiritual body of believers in Christ. Close your eyes for a moment and visualize your physical body as being composed of only eyes. Suddenly hands would become eyes, feet would become eyes — the entire body would become eyes. At the same time other people in your family would become all ears . . . or all toes . . . or all lungs. What a hopeless mess our lives would be if we had been so designed. There could never be a completeness of independence. How incredibly perfect our God has designed the complementary components of our physical bodies.

In spiritual relationships it is exciting to welcome the different gifts God has placed in the body of Christ, for they work together for the common good or the completion and perfection of that body and its function. In 1 Corinthians 12:28 we discover that "In the church (the body of Christ) God has appointed first of all apostles, second prophets, third teachers, then workers of miracles, also those having gifts of healing, those able to help others, those with gifts of administration, and finally those speaking in different kinds of tongues."

God has placed top priority on getting out the riches of the depths of His Word, for all other ministries are dependent upon the proclamation of what God has said. We do not need counselors if they have no wisdom of God's concepts as revealed through the Bible. Our culture today reflects the work of counselors who

110

are limited to the knowledge of men, and often that work is in open opposition to the true principles of God. Without the message of God there is no direction for living now or eternally. No wonder that He has placed the primary emphasis on these proclamative gifts. After them come the supportive gifts of healing, helping, and others. In each scriptural passage on gifts, God lists last the gift of tongues and the interpretation of tongues. Yet today man seems to have turned those priorities around. The Bible says, "The highest gift you can wish for is to be able to speak the messages of God" (1 Cor. 14:1, PHILLIPS). And the remainder of that chapter deals with the dangers of emphasizing the gift of tongues instead of the gifts directly related to the preaching-teaching ministry. Yet the gift of tongues has become the most sought-after, controversial gift of all!

I have many dear friends whom I value highly who tell me they have the gift of tongues. Some of the richest prayer support I have ever known has been through their ministry, and I have spoken in their churches. But I do not have the gift of tongues nor am I looking for it. God has clearly stated that not all people will have the gift of tongues or any other one particular gift. I am not spiritually inferior because I do not have this gift. Jesus Christ died for me just as He did for my friends to whom He has given this gift. He loves me and He loves them; neither of us is spiritually inferior. But we are *different* with different gifts for the completing of the entire body of Christ.

The gift of tongues or the gift of healing do not in any way imply spiritual maturity; they are simply God's choice for the person who possesses them. One does not become spiritually mature suddenly, nor does one become good enough to receive a gift as a reward for goodness. A gift is an *unearned* present or it is not a gift at all.

Here in Southern California, I have people stop by in their door-to-door cult activity. As an evidence of their right to heaven they tell me that they have attended so many lectures of their leaders, that they have participated in so many witness campaigns, etc. In their religious program they are frantically working their way up the ladder of God's good grace. But God explicitly states, "For it is by grace (the unearned favor and kindness of God) you have been saved, through faith — and this is not from yourselves, it is the *gift* of God — not by works, so that no one can boast" (Eph. 2:8,9, italics mine). The gift of salvation through which every person who is a part of the body of Christ must come into that body is a free gift. It cost God a great deal — the giving of His Son Jesus Christ to pay the penalty for our sin — but to us it is a totally unearned, undeserved gift. It is a gift of God's grace.

In the original Greek of the New Testament, many of the references translated "gift" are from the word *charisma*, meaning a gift of grace. This places emphasis upon the fact that God is the Giver and that the gift itself is entirely of His grace or undeserved favor.

Years ago Charles Spurgeon said, "I looked to God and the dove of peace flew into my heart. I looked at the peace and the dove flew away." How often I have looked to God in times of need and deep longing and He has brought His warm peace and solutions. Then as I hugged those treasured moments to myself and looked at the gift of peace or His activity on my behalf, slowly I discovered that my little treasure had become tarnished and no longer lovely or practical. At times it has even become a point of guilt. When I have found myself measuring that moment in my life by the yardstick of past high points of fellowship with Jesus, then I have realized that "the dove" has flown away. It is the focus of attention upon Jesus Christ and Him alone that ushers in the dove of peace, the cascade of joy, and the strength that it generates. The joy of the experience is just an added benefit to us, but it is Christ who should be the focus of our attention.

The use of every spiritual gift can generate the peace and joy of the Spirit of God operating through that gift, or it can produce conflict and tension if man is dominating and seeking to control the gift. The results depend upon the one who is in control. A good test to determine whether God is directing the use of a gift is to examine the results of its use, and this brings us to the third guideline in considering the use of spiritual gifts:

3) What are the results of the use of this particular gift?

In today's instamatic age most of us look for shortcuts, ways to do things more quickly and cheaply. We would even like to speed up growth processes at times and make them as painless as possible. In our highly competitive society it would seem humanly logical that if a person could do certain spiritual activities, he would reflect growth and maturity. But gifts are not a barometer by which to measure spirituality.

Quality of life is measured by the fruit the life produces. When I was in Florida recently, I passed some orange trees. I noticed that some small, young trees were bearing fruit. The oranges were tiny, but they were oranges. Just behind them stood a grove of older trees heavy with large, beautiful oranges. They were more fully developed, and their fruit reflected that development. "The Spirit, however, produces in human life fruits such as these: love, joy, peace, patience, kindness, generosity, fidelity, tolerance and self control — and no law exists against any of them" (Gal. 5:22-23, PHILLIPS).

The Spirit of God at work in a life that is completely open and yielded to Him produces a beautiful crop of fruit. The person who has just come to Jesus Christ may not yet have grown and matured in the knowledge of Christ's loving activity in all areas of his life and, therefore, may not have all his spiritual fruit developed yet. But God will be faithful to lead him on to greater and richer development and fruit-bearing.

God gives us the only valid shortcut to spiritual maturity, and it is found in the thirteenth chapter of 1 Corinthians. It is the beautiful unfolding of genuine love that is the power behind the use of each of the spiritual gifts; without that love, none of them have positive value. Chapter fourteen contains this challenge: "Follow, then, the way of love, while you set your heart on the gifts of the Spirit" (1 Cor. 14:1, PHILLIPS).

How can I get the gift I want? It's simple! "Delight thyself also in the Lord; and he shall give thee the desires of thine heart" (Ps. 37:4). Is your delight in Jesus Christ? Do you want what He wants for you? Then you can be sure you will receive that which God desires for you! If you want anything less than God has in mind, allow Him to show you the joy of discovering His better purpose, plan, and gifts, for there is where your true happiness will be.

The God who can count the apples in a seed can flood the inner tomb of our life where His gifts lie hidden, waiting the life-giving warmth of the Son-light of His love. The power who turned on the sun in the dark eons before creation's dawn can germinate the seed-gift He has planted in the good soil of our lives. Who can measure the impact and harvest of the use of those gifts as they produce fruit in the lives of all with whom we come in contact? The cycle moves on gathering force and discovering new seeds.

The seed of the eternal life of God is planted in those who respond to His gift of Jesus Christ — Jesus Christ, who left a tomb almost 2,000 years ago to return to the treasury of heaven, but not without leaving His deposit in life here and now. Welcome the gifts and the Giver so He may enjoy living again in His beautiful body — the body of believers. "That the body should work together as a whole with all the members in sympathetic relationship with one another."

Do you hear Him at your door just now as He knocks and waits for you to make your home His home? There He will reveal how to become free in the family.

Free
in the Family

I WILL give you $100,000
for your child," Miss Molly said. It was not an idle offer
for she had the financial capability to make it good.

I don't remember much about the lonely old
woman except that she had survived three husbands,
amassing a fortune from each one. She had long since
dismissed all servants except the groundskeeper who
was never permitted to enter the main house — nor
were her attorneys, doctors, or deliverymen who com-
prised her entire world of contacts. None were trusted,
nor were banks. Dirty little tobacco sacks containing
expensive jewelry were hidden inside mattress covers.

Only her Siamese cat had unrestricted freedom to roam the house.

It was quite a house with leaded and stained-glass windows. As a child I loved to try to capture the red and purple rays of late afternoon sunshine as they danced across walls and carpets. But I could never hang on to the prisms of color. All too soon they were gone, and the drabness of the old mansion settled into gloom and darkness of night.

I'm not sure how we met Miss Molly or what her motivation was for having us stay with her. Perhaps her overwhelming loneliness or fear of fire and death prompted her to have someone near her again. When the day came that we were to leave, she made this incredible offer to my parents. She wanted to buy a child, an heir, for she had none. Perhaps she really wanted to buy a reason for living, a sense of having a family even though it was just a child. Perhaps a child could be trusted, and certainly it could love back more effectively than a cat!

Everybody needs somebody to love back, someone with whom they identify and to whom they belong. Yet in the complexity of human need the pendulum swings wide from this longing to the need to be a free person.

All forms of life have their beginning in the struggle for freedom. A tiny green shoot bursts the embryonic seed to become an individual plant. Plant and animal life bear a strong parallel to the life of man. The desire to be free is first expressed in the birth pangs of release even before a child is born. As the umbilical cord is severed, the outraged cry is heard — a cry that is the reaction to change. The warm security of the womb is gone; the oxygen of independence is breathed in.

From that moment each life is totally absorbed in physical self-discovery. Sensations of hunger, wetness, cold, or discomfort produce demands to have those needs met. Demands that need no words for expression or understanding.

As needs are met, discovery moves on to the fascination with the intricate mechanism of fingers, toes, and eventually the infant's entire world. The physical birth places top priority on understanding how to use physical equipment in a material world. Survival demands that fingers guide food to the mouth, but *selective choice* determines which foods. Hopefully, worms are rejected for more tasty nutritious morsels. The highchair decor may be spinach green or squash gold, but the cry of independence will be heard loud and clear. The message is simply, "This is your choice. It is not *my* choice. I am willing to fight for the right to choose."

Discovery and selective choice are two of the basic elements of life and personality. If there is to be mental and physical health, freedom and happiness, there must be continual opportunity for new discovery. Each discovery brings selective choice into full focus as the individual decides how that discovery will affect his actions, attitudes, and feelings about self, others, and environment. It is the basis for true maturity.

A child is quick to discover imperfect features, and the unconscious choice is then made to use that feature as a positive motivation or a negative excuse and barrier to becoming a free person.

I learned early in life that having a hairline I disliked was a challenge to develop nice hair-styles. But I also detested the space between my front teeth. For a while I refused to smile and was on my way to becom-

119

ing a dour person. One day my mother's friend said, "June, you have such a delightful smile. Your dimples are just beautiful."

Soon I discovered that people were not absorbed with my imperfect teeth. In fact, it seemed to make no difference to anyone. People liked me even though I was not flawless. My natural smile was back to stay, and I was freed from that childish fear of rejection because of imperfection. I am grateful for the kind words of a wise woman who encouraged me to focus on good points instead of attempting to hide my flaws. I have discovered that it is when I try to hide my personal imperfections that I am most limited. As I concentrate on them, my energy, time, and creative ability are being absorbed in a uselsss charade that produces new fears of rejection: Will someone discover my secret?

Discoveries of self flow from the beginning to the end of life. The approach of legal adulthood can be a shattering or thrilling time. Graduation closes the door to certain activities and friendships, but it opens a new door to a wider variety of experiences and relationships. It is selective choice that determines whether one will concentrate on the gains or the losses. The person who has built a habit of seeing only personal flaws and imperfections will find it difficult to choose to look for things gained. The security of old friendships and activities will offer strong temptation to reject the possibility of increased opportunity. The unknown can become frightening.

Last year, following a seminar at a Washington college, a high school senior shared her struggle with me. She desperately wanted to become involved in the medical profession and had been offered an opportunity for training with a salaried job. It would have been possible for her to earn much-needed money while she was preparing for her career. But she was afraid she might not make it in the new situation . . . people might not like her. She had turned down the offer and decided to stay with her parents and help care for a semi-invalid father. It was not the desire or need of her family to have her stay with them. It simply offered an escape from facing the insecurity she felt in a new situation. Growth comes by stretching the muscles of our body and mind as well as our potential. Greater achievements always demand an investment of time, creativity, and self. Then we expand our total self to new dimensions and enjoy the gains.

Being almost eighteen, forty, sixty-five, or eighty have much the same emotional impact. At forty the focus is slightly different; there is that shaky feeling of wondering how much longer one is needed, wanted. Being almost sixty-five or even eighty brings a brand-new crop of uncertainties. It's the *almost* that alerts us to the fact that here is an unknown area of life to conquer — or be conquered by it.

It is not the aging process that threatens us as much as the possibility of changed relationships, opportunities, and even locations. We question, "Will retirement benefits enable us to maintain our living standard and financial independence? Will we be forced to leave this home with its memories of births and marriages? Will our opinions still have value to our children? Will they care enough to spend time with us?"

But all these things have to do with the backward look and are *loss*-centered. When new discoveries are in full view, we are able to think in terms of gains; *now* is the time to develop new creative abilities that have

121

not been possible during the pressurized days of raising a family. Art, music, hobbies, assistance in research programs that need the knowledge and wisdom of experience, service to the blind or to physically handicapped people, and scores of other activities and interests swing open the door to stimulating productivity and creativity in new fields.

We must choose to free ourselves from the debilitating fear of loss to embrace liberating discoveries of an expanding life. Discovery and selective choice are as available at eighty as they were in the highchair!

The potential to be free is wrapped up in the discovery of understanding the longings we feel and how to effectively satisfy them in a positive expansion of the use of talents and gifts. And it is the harmonizing of the longing for personal liberation and the desire to belong to someone that enriches life in the home.

The family drive is as basic as breathing, and it is no less strong today than it was 6,000 years ago! There has been an attempt at substitution in recent years, but the desire for small group living is increasing with current pressures and uncertainties. Communal living, open marriage, and evolving life styles carry a big message if anybody is listening. It is the attempt to harmonize the need for the security of identification with a family group and at the same time reserve the feeling of freedom by abstention from binding commitment.

Ironically enough there is no real security of belonging without commitment. Open or trial "marriage" is not simply marriage without the legal involvement of a piece of paper. It is a withholding of a three-way commitment, a reservation of giving of one's self to a person with whom life is to be shared, on the basis of the possibility that it might not work out. It is to *anticipate* an *inability* to *succeed* in life's most privileged human relationship and to allow for that failure. The successfulness of any marriage can be gauged to a large degree by these three commitments:

1) The commitment of two people to each other.

The giving side of commitment has been stressed so much that it has blinded us largely to the *receiving* side of commitment which is even more important. A penetrating consideration lies in our personal answer to this question: "Am I prepared to receive or accept that which my marriage partner has to offer? Can I accept his sexuality?"

It has been said by someone that a man's release seems to be in sex. He does not see a sexual interlude as the result of a romantic build-up, but is ready for it when he's mad, sad, bad, or glad. A woman welcomes sexual intercourse as the conclusion to lovemaking. The setting and timing must be right; it must be romantic. Is a woman ready to accept this radically different concept of relationship? Is a man willing to fulfill the need of a woman for the romantic build-up that is important to her emotional gratification?

Are we willing to receive or accept the individuality of temperament, of attitudes that are different from ours, of special interests in sports, hobbies, and entertainment that may even be opposed to ours? Are we prepared to accept different political and social expressions of living? Different financial standards and uses of time and money? All of these and many other areas of individuality bring *input* into our life, and personal commitment to a marriage partner involves the willingness to *accept that input*. It is the rejection or attempt to change that input that builds conflict and loss of relationship.

Commitment is a two-way street of input and output. The giving of self in the sheer joy of giving love and the spirit of moving to meet needs in the life of another person represents a part of output. Commitment also respects the right of that person to give in return, physically, emotionally, mentally, and spiritually, and exhibits a willingness to accept that input.

Perhaps we need to add this footnote to the marriage vows: "I do not expect you to agree with me, to think, talk, do, and feel as I do, for you are not me. I love you because you are you. I do not need or want two of me, so I shall welcome all the variety of ingredients of your personality, for in doing so I welcome you."

2) Commitment to the relationship of marriage itself.

Marriage is not a "Try it, you'll like it" or "Try it, and if you don't like it, dissolve it" affair. If you don't like it, find out why it isn't working and do something about it. Marriage itself does not make anyone sad or happy, a success or a failure. But it does turn the floodlight on weaknesses in personal attitudes, and by bringing them to the surface enables a person to recognize and overcome them.

Anytime two or more people enter into a relationship where different habits and viewpoints are to be shared, there will be growth or conflict. Conflict is the result of an unwillingness to think, react, or respond beyond our ordinary pattern. It is a state of mind that depends on some form of opposition. Most marriage conflicts could be resolved if the two people who have committed themselves to each other placed enough value on the institution of marriage and the home to calmly sit down and honestly talk about the patterns of conflict in their relationship. It is essential to a) determine what the actual problem is and the logical, common-sense way of solving it; b) agree on the portion of responsibility that each person will take; c) and help each other to follow through in maintaining individual responsibility. To throw in the towel because there is conflict is to carry the same thought and habit patterns into future relationship and build them again in similar situations. All marriages have conflicts, but good marriages result when the conflicts are solved by the partners working together.

3) The commitment of marriage partners to God in the home.

Can a marriage be successful without God? Would a Ford be a Ford without Henry? There is no school or expert that can tell you exactly what to say and do in every situation to produce a perfect marriage, mainly because there are no perfect marriages. In order to have a perfect marriage it would require two perfect people, and there just aren't any around. Even if there were such a possibility, the chances of two of them finding each other and getting together in marriage would be mighty small.

There are a lot of marriages that seem to be doing all right without God, but if you observe them long enough you will discover tremendous needs over a period of a few years. Those that seem great today may be dissolved next year. The simple fact is that sooner or later all of us need help in having happier, better marriages. Since God is the manufacturer of people and marriages (He gave the first bride away in the Garden wedding, to say nothing of having designed her and the groom!), His blueprint for the happy family is especially valuable. Provision has been made in that plan for the specific use of natural talents, supernatural gifts, and enjoyment of the blending of temperaments into one harmonious whole. *Every lack of harmony is the outward evidence of inward deviation from that plan.*

The ideal family unit is based on a man and a woman who care about each other and have committed themselves to each other, to the development of the marriage relationship, and ultimately to God. Certainly there are variations of this ideal basic unit, and even in the ideal beginning there will be different opinions and solutions to current problems. Where there are different views, there must be one authority who takes responsibility for the final decisions as in the case of the chairman of the board in a corporate structure. God has given that role to the husband if there is a husband in the family. It has nothing to do with his ability or rightness, but is an accountability and administrative authority for the well-being of all in that family. The wife and children are to bring the full resources of their ideas, likes and dislikes, talents, and gifts into the pool of family resources, and it is the final decision of the husband and father to gratefully acknowledge and determine the best use of their contribution.

It is not the purpose of this book to develop an in-depth teaching on marriage relationships, for I have written a great deal about them in my books *Why Sink When You Can Swim?* and *The God of the Impossible.* But it is my desire to show family relationships as a part of a total life concept. For the structure of the family is deeply interwoven in eternity itself and is in fact the training ground for life beyond the grave.

The physical family, the present representation of

the spiritual family, and the eternal family of God have as definite a relationship to one another as do body, soul, and spirit in forming the unity of the individual person.

Life in the Family of the Future

Because of the final purposes of life, it is important to catch a glimpse of life as it will be. The open door through which we see it revealed is the Bible. There we find that eternity is not an endless floating on a rosy cloud replete with harp-playing and idleness. It is going to be filled with fantastic activity. If you like music, the concerts are going to be incredible! If you find your particular stimulus in organization and managerial activity, you will certainly be in the seventh heaven, for the Bible says we shall one day rule with Christ! If you're a connoisseur of good food, you're in for great enjoyment. If you're a nature lover, you're not left out. The Bible speaks of a specific place with a river, trees, and fruit and many other things. The gemologist will have a heyday, for in all the mines of gemstones and precious metals on earth today there is nothing to compare to the incredible wealth and beauty of the display of these things that are actually used as building materials in the eternal city! The Bible also reveals that there will be no negative feelings or influences there; no pain, tears, sorrow, separation, fear, sin, or death.

In view of these marvelous changes planned by the same God who designed this earth, it is important that those who are to breathe the eternal atmosphere of such a liberated life be prepared for it. The training program for that future dimension is here and now. One phase is through the physical family and relationships of people learning to live happily together. The second phase is through the activity of the spiritual body of Christ as those members interact with each other in the institution of the local church, for it is the earthly representation of the family of God regardless of the denominational banner flying over it.

Not all church organizations are a part of that spiritual body, for those who make up the constituency of some churches have had no personal commitment to Jesus Christ. Indeed, some so-called churches today are dedicated to the worship of Satan. But the organizational church, composed of individuals who have received the forgiveness of sin through the death and resurrection of Christ, is the physical reality of the spiritual family of God among men today.

God's commands for this church as well as for the administrative leadership and many other important areas of life in the human family are designed by Him to prepare the individual for happy successful living here and now and for life as it shall be in eternity.

As children learn respectful obedience to parents and as wives adapt plans and activities to the counsel of their husbands, they become free of unnecessary responsibilities — responsibilities God has not given them. Through this they learn to respectfully acknowledge and adjust to God's direction now and for eternity. His commands will direct all functions then, and this is an opportunity to learn the joyful freeing result of adjusting to them now. When we do so, God Himself takes the responsibility for the final results, for He will never allow faith and confidence that prompts obedience to be the loser. We may go through difficult days along the way, but even those seemingly harsh happenings will bring worthwhile positive results in the life that is firmly relying on God. God does not deliver us from dishes and diapers, long hours and tedious details, but He does deliver us from our reactions against them!

It is important in the family relationship to help each person see the success he can become. The key to actually becoming that person is in the recognition of natural talents and spiritual gifts. A primary goal of every parent should be to help each child as well as the marriage partner discover these powerful means of fulfillment and to implement projects, training, and other means of encouraging the full use of these assets daily as well as in the future.

Happiness is dependent upon self-worth and the ability to feel worthwhile accomplishment. Sometimes we tackle such a major task that we become exhausted in the daily grind of seeing it through. Try finding some small thing each day that reflects positive value in personal achievement. It may be writing a letter to encourage someone, doing an errand for a neighbor, or helping a child to overcome discouragement. Who can determine the value of small or great kindnesses?

This is equally true in the church. The building of spiritually healthy families multiplies the outreach and successful ministry of any local church. The impact of those homes on the church and the community is a positive reflection on lives who need Christ.

There is no limit to what God can do when we bring ourselves to the greatest commitment of all . . . the willingness to become the person whom God designed us to be. Is liberation to be found in Women's Lib? Men's Lib? Children's Lib? There is only one total liberation movement. The liberated life under the directive headship of the Master Designer — Jesus Christ!

Have you been liberated? Are you running free? Jesus invites you to join Him who knew what it was to walk through death and come out free from the bondage of graveclothes and tomb. The Giver of Gifts has given Himself *for* you and *to* you today.

May He grant you out of the rich treasury of His glory to be strengthened *and* reinforced with mighty power in the inner man by the (Holy) Spirit [Himself] — indwelling your innermost being and personality. May Christ through your faith [actually] dwell — settle down, abide, make His permanent home — in your hearts! (Eph. 3:16,17, AMPLIFIED BIBLE).

Free to Be Me

THE lights went out as the operator locked the door of the beauty salon behind us. Making my way down the escalator alone, I was amazed at the seemingly deserted floors of the large downtown department store. I knew the city was in a major recession, but I did not realize that business was this bad! As I reached the fourth floor, towering rolls of carpet loomed above me like threatening sentries. Never had I seen the upper stories of this beautiful store so dark. Seconds later, between floors, the escalator slithered to a silent stop. With quickening steps I hurried to the first floor. My throat tightened with a sudden choking sensation: "I couldn't possibly be locked in this store. It's still ten minutes until closing time!" My feet hurried to catch up with my pulse as I shook each door without results. There must be an emergency number. They just couldn't do this to me! But they had! I was locked in and alone.

I glanced without interest at the gorgeous fur coats, diamond rings, and counters full of other delectable taste-teasers. There was a time when I would have turned handsprings to rummage through all those treasures undisturbed, but now all I wanted was *out!* With knocking knees and sweating hands I made my way to the center of the floor. What a huge store! Suddenly my usually well-developed voice seemed to have a maximum performance level of a faint whisper: "Is anybody here?" My words seemed to catch the rhythm of ghostly figures chasing me from the reflections of nearby neon signs.

Searching for courage to speak above my queasy stomach, I repeated, "Is anybody here?" The silence bounced back painfully. With a rising mixture of panic and determination, I screamed as loud as I could, "Is anybody here! . . . If you are, you had better answer me!"

Maybe it was the threatening tone that did it, or the perception of the maintenance man, but the beautiful sound of a human voice drifted back to me over the vast expanse of showcases. "Lady, what are you doing here? Don't you know this store has been closed for over thirty minutes?" I guess my obvious ignorance of the store's new closing hours penetrated his established routine, and in kindly benevolence he said, "Well, come on over here and I'll show you the way out."

I must confess I did not look to see how that man

parted his hair or tied his shoes. I don't even know if his skin was red, purple, black, or white — and I couldn't have cared less. He had what I needed — the knowledge and the keys of release. He knew how to get me out of this locked-in situation.

Several years ago a desperate lady came to my home. Her husband was having an affair, and she had abundant problems with her children, her finances, and her health. My son greeted her at the door and welcomed her into our home. She took one look at his hair that gently cupped his earlobes and ended well above the collar. Hurriedly she excused herself, for she felt that I couldn't possibly be of help to her if my son wore his hair in a way she did not approve of. In righteous defense of my son I must say he looked far better that way than he ever had when it was clipped above his ears. It was neat and immaculate, but it did not agree with the lady's standards.

That dear woman continues to have difficulties, not because she and I did not get together, but because life and the people who make up her daily experience simply do not conform to her opinion of what they should be, say, and do. I think of this woman's needless suffering often, and my heart goes out to all who are caught in the trap of loneliness, sadness, and depression; for many times it is increased if not caused by our sense of disappointment, loss, and frustration.

Alone or Lonely

Loneliness is America's number-one disease today. There is an ever-increasing number of people who are living alone, but being alone does not necessarily cause or have anything to do with being lonely! Recently I was in New York's Grand Central Station, and

133

I was amazed at the expressions of the early-morning commuters. Their faces looked as desperate as the Las Vegas tourist-gamblers on a Labor Day weekend. I watched as they obtained tickets from a machine and coffee from a dispenser; if any conversation took place it was over a phone. The scene was cold, dehumanized, and mechanical. I wandered into a tiny stall of a donut shop and suddenly my whole world changed. A beautiful, beaming black lady said a cheery, "Good morning!" We talked over my coffee and donuts, and when I left she wished me "a happy day." I saw thousands of people that day, but her face is the only face I remember. She invested her time and interest in speaking personally to me — a stranger whom she did not know and would probably never see again. I was just a traveler passing through, but she made me feel special and cared for.

We are daily travelers, though we may not take a subway. Each day we travel a little farther on the road of life. Most of us ask, at times, if the mad rush is worth it. Then some fellow traveler breaks the dull pattern of nothingness — he may smile or speak or share an encouraging thought or the fleeting touch of a warm human hand. He is a person as we are, and he has needs too. At times I think, "O God, don't let me wait for someone else to show friendliness; let me be the first. Lord, you know I'm selfish. If they show friendliness to me first, You will reward them. Right about now I need Your rewards. Let me be the first to speak, to love, to care. How about it, Lord; who's next today?"

There is no shortage of people with needs. They are like swirling seas that engulf us on every side: at the market there are the cashier, the butcher, and the bag boy or girl (sometimes I can't tell which is which).

There are lonely people who pump gas in the gas station, who handle our clothes at the dry cleaners, deliverymen who pound at the door, phone solicitors who even get hold of unlisted numbers. God has planted us in the midst of this area of ministry, this world of lonely people. But the biggest field of all is the people we live with in our own homes.

The American family scene has changed radically in recent years. Many of us are living with interesting "strangers" whom we find dull and boring. We have simply never taken time to get acquainted. Three families recently shared their experiences with me. Marge and Harry are about fifty and have been married thirty years. Friends looked at them and said, "What an ideal marriage. They are perfect together." But recently Harry left home without warning. Finally Marge located him through the local police. When confronted with his sudden exodus, Harry said, "I had to find out if she knew I was there or not. When I'm home she eats and watches TV, and I just wasn't sure she would realize I was gone until the groceries ran out. Is there anything to eat at home?"

Christine and Thad are about thirty-five and have been married nine years. She is staying with a friend while job hunting. Does she need to work? Absolutely not! Thad owns a flourishing business, and she has a generous budget to allow for travel and just about anything else she chooses to do. But she says, "Thad doesn't want me involved in his business. I am not to come around the office. When he is at home, the minute dinner is over it's TV baseball, football, and just for variety a hockey game or tennis (on TV of course). I simply do not exist as a person who has ideas and interests or value. I am as automatic as an elevator.

As long as he can push a button and get an answer, I will never be a real-live person. I have nothing to contribute but occasional sex. If I don't do something now, I will spend the next forty years as a vegetable. I wouldn't even make a good vegetable, for at least an onion can evoke tears."

Then there is Judy who is just seventeen. When her parents came to the detention home to visit her, she said, "Why did you come to talk to me here? You were never interested when I was at home!"

What are all these people and millions like them saying? "I am lonely! I am not important in my family. Who needs me or really cares about me as a person? Who wants to listen to me?"

Organizations who treat people involved in destructive excesses of alcohol, food, drugs, and sex find one common cause in most cases. Regardless of financial resources, social status, racial or religious backgrounds, age, or sex, loneliness pervades.

Causes and Cures

There are several specific reasons for loneliness, and before we move to the simple solution, let's take a look at the causes. Our life style in the United States is a major factor contributing to loneliness. Recently I was in Cairo, and after breakfast I waved good-by to the African continent. Soon afterward I landed in Istanbul, which is the only city in the world that spans two continents, both Europe and Asia. During the lovely lunch at Topkapi Palace I realized that I had been on three continents that morning! At other times I have driven through Syria, Lebanon, Jordan, and Israel in a matter of hours. But here in America we may drive for days to visit a relative in another state! We are swallowed up in the immensity of land masses and distances. By contrast, the mechanized life in metropolitan areas, such as the situation in Grand Central Station, builds feelings of loneliness. We feel, "No one has time for me or cares. . . . I am nobody. . . . I have no meaningful identity."

Perhaps our country has offered less stabilizing family ties than have most European or Asiatic countries. We are a new nation still in our infancy and have not stressed the value of being Joe Jones' son or Tom Smith's grandson unless that ancestor happened to be a national figure. We are also a nation of people on the move, and often children grow up without ever having known the security of grandparents. Our five children have never had this privilege, so as a family we have "adopted grandparents" from among our neighbors who have had no nearby grandchildren to enjoy. It became an interesting two-way street of meeting the needs of older friends as well as those of our children.

Perhaps the greatest single reason for the sense of loneliness today springs from our concept of being alone. We have glanced briefly at the impact of temperaments, especially in relationship to children in their outlook on playing or being alone. Many adults have been programed since childhood to believe that it is unnatural and unhealthy to be alone, while nothing is further from the truth.

I thoroughly enjoy people. I love to be with them and to do things with them. But some of my most prized days are those I have spent alone. There are so many things that cannot be accomplished unless a person is alone. Creative writing, painting, musical composition, and a host of other creative interests demand solitude. Then there are those special experiences: I enjoy walking in the breaking edge of the surf, feeling the silvery sand squeeze between my toes and the crisp halo of spray falling around my shoulders like a mantle. I thrill to the brilliant blaze of sunset as it softens the edge of purple mountains, and I feel that inner exhilaration as I sense God's presence wrapping me in His love. "O God, how can I say thank You for such a fantastic world and for putting me in this particular place at this moment!" I am alone and it is marvelous!

Someone might say, "That's okay for you — you've got it together and your life's working out." Dear person, I don't have it all together. I simply know a God who does, and He is the same One who waits to put it all together for you. Don't be afraid to be quiet for a few minutes to be alone with Him. I think my life without God would have been a miserable existence. There have been a lot of problems that hurt. Cancer, a debilitating auto accident, as well as total financial losses, to say nothing of our unplanned, accidental wedding. There have been many lonely, teary nights when Hal has been away and I have struggled through the highs and lows of bringing five teen-agers to adulthood. (I hope they have arrived!) But God has been the great plus that has changed every negative loss into a positive gain. I am the gal who has fought, cried, laughed, and sighed through it all only to discover God was there with me every step and every moment.

If you are alone today, regardless of the reasons, have you looked at the plus side of your life? For the person who lives alone, there is freedom to choose independently how to use money, time, and resources; freedom to choose how and when to dress, eat, travel, study, play, and work, and most of all unrestricted freedom to be totally available to God. Years ago my friend Henrietta Mears broke her engagement to a charming young man and chose to live alone so she might be totally free to have God work through her life to meet the needs of others. And He did! She is credited with having channeled and challenged thousands of young men and women into pulpits and missionary activity, and in addition she founded Gospel Light Press.

It isn't how many hours, days, or years we spend alone, it is what we *do* during that time that makes the difference. Loneliness cannot possibly flourish unless a person chooses to do these four things: (1) concentrate on losses and think often of the way life used to be; (2) feel sorry for self thinking life should have been easier, better, richer, happier; (3) wait on others to meet needs; and (4) resent people who fail to do so.

Healing loneliness is simply a matter of reversing those four steps and walking out into happy, free involvement. If you have been locked into the loneliness syndrome, it's time to enjoy release. As an aid to changing negative thought patterns to positive, make a list of a personal gain for every loss you can think of. You will be amazed at the resources you have to work with.

My dearest friend, Pearl King, has known many losses. A few years ago her husband died tragically and unexpectedly. Shortly after, her father who lived with her and had been very close to her went to his heavenly home. Then her little dog was taken from her, and she was left seemingly alone. Yet at the peak of her losses she chose to search for positive uses of those things she had left.

Today her guest room is seldom vacant, and fortunate is the person who shares her bright companionship and warm hospitality. Her home is filled with colorful flowers and beauty. She buys dog food by the hundred-pound sack to feed the racoons who scratch at her kitchen door if she is late with their feeding. I have watched ten to fifteen of these little creatures at a time gather for their evening meal beneath the huge tree that shadows her patio. On those rare evenings when she dines at home alone, she chooses from a wide assortment of various colored place settings. Pearl is a fabulous cook, and whether alone or preparing dinner for guests she will use no canned food. She is known and loved across America as she organizes retreats for Winning Women and shares her tremendous message. You see, much of it was *developed out of losses that have become gains*. Is Pearl alone? Never! No person is ever totally alone.

Psalm 139 says,

> O Lord, you . . . know everything about me. You know when I sit or stand. When far away you know my every thought. You chart the path ahead of me, and tell me where to stop and rest. Every moment, you know where I am. You know what I am going to say before I even say it. You both precede and follow me, and place your hand of blessing on my head. This is too glorious, too wonderful to believe! I can *never* be lost to your Spirit! I can *never* get away from my God! If I go up to heaven, you are there; if I go down to the place of the dead, you are there. If I ride the morning winds to the farthest oceans, even there your hand will guide me, your strength will support me. If I try to hide in darkness, the night becomes light around me. For even darkness cannot hide from God; to you the night shines as bright as day. Darkness and light are both alike to you (LB).

You are loved by at least one Person at all times, no matter where you are or what you are doing or have done. God says, "Yea, I have loved thee with an ever-lasting love: therefore with lovingkindness have I drawn thee" (Jer. 31:3). It is that love that makes forgiveness possible through the death and resurrection of Jesus Christ His own dear Son. Jesus did not die so the world might have a nice story to tell, but that you might have the abundant life of God within you through receiving Christ into your heart and life. Then you have the assurances that He shares that empty bed or chair. And because He is vitally alive to you, you have something of practical reality to share with others. There will always be losses and gains, and we may choose to develop one or the other.

Jill Renich writes Christian best sellers today. She is also the founder of Winning Women, an organization that twice each year hosts as many as 5,000 women at its various retreats. But there was a time a few years ago when Jill was a lonely woman. She had moved to a new area and in the loneliness of her apartment decided that there must be other women like herself who were also lonely. She baked a cake and began knocking on doors of strangers inviting them to come and enjoy her cake with her. They came and she shared a few encouraging verses of God's Word from the Bible with them. One of the women said, "This has been so wonderful. Next week I will bake the cake if you will all come and share it with me." Soon a full-fledged Bible study developed and ultimately an international ministry.

From tiny seeds of friendliness grew a great work, and today I wonder what God will do with the seeds you plant? The kind of seeds you choose to sow determine the life you will ultimately grow. Seeds of self-pity grow loneliness, whereas seeds of friendly kindness grow friendship, warmth, and love. Sow your life with the crop you want to live with each day, for you will have to live with the results.

Jill did not wait for neighbors to call but concentrated on being the good neighbor. If she had waited for others to meet her needs, she would probably be a lonely woman today. Neither she nor Pearl nor anyone else I have ever met who has a dynamic message and life has allowed herself to indulge in the waste of self-pity. That is a retreat into self, isolating us from those who care. And it leads us to resent those who do not come up to our standards or expectations, especially in meeting our needs.

I am convinced that millions of people who do not live alone but who are desperately lonely in their family relationships are living on the fine edge of a beautiful adventure. Loneliness is a *feeling* that results from the misuse of a tremendous asset. If you are lonely, it is the sure evidence that you have a great capacity for friendship, for loving and giving to others, for identification with people. When you are not actually involved in doing so, you *feel the loss of not using your capacity*; and that is exactly the emotion we diagnose as loneliness. It is the unused ability to give happiness to others and thereby to enjoy the same thing yourself.

There is a marvelous way to get a free face-lift *today* that actually changes the lines in one's physical face. It is the simple art of smiling at others, especially in the family circle. A smile that says, "I *care* about you. I *care* what happens to you today at work, at school, in the house, or in the church. You are important to me, and you are important to my God. What do you need most that *I* can do for you today? Wash a shirt? Clean the garage? Fix a leaky faucet?" Maybe it's just not mentioning that the toothpaste tube is squeezed out of shape again; maybe it's to be available to listen, to hear others and find out what they are really like inside.

Why is it that people join clubs and organizations to have someone to talk to, to be involved with? Could it possibly be that relationships in the home have become so dull that if one is to stay awake he or she must find someone outside of the home to share his or her evening? Could it be that in the home we have lost the fine art of showing appreciation and gratitude for each other or of sharing the deep inner person with one another? Many homes are made up of strangers struggling together in defensive living.

I have noticed that clubs have a way of getting to know the inner person quickly. They have simple questionnaires, which are filled out and circulated among the group so that each person can begin to know another. Questions include personal likes and special interests of the individual; for example, "What is your favorite food, recreation, form of entertainment, sport, hobby, state, town, or country, national park, or holiday? How would you prefer to spend your vacation, your day off, or extra money? If you could begin a new career *today*, what would you choose to do?" All of these are like small roads that lead us to the inner person.

Let me ask you a question: If you were to attempt to answer every one of the above questions about each person in your home, how many of your answers do you think would be absolutely correct? In recent tests it has been discovered that most husbands and wives do not get 25 percent of those questions right about each other! We have an opinion about the man or woman we live with, but all too often it is *our* version of his or her favorite things rather than his or her own personal choice.

Scores of people are lonely in their family relationships today because they do not open their lives to each other. It is easy to become involved in defensive shadowboxing with an image that does not exist; or if it does, it is all too often manufactured through faulty evaluation of others. I am so glad that Pearl and Jill and countless other individuals have not allowed loneliness to become a permanent way of life; if they had done so, the world would be much poorer today.

Everyone has temporary periods of loneliness, and often that empty feeling is the spirit's longing for the warm companionship of Jesus Christ Himself. It is a desire that all the people in the world cannot adequately satisfy. Jesus Himself experienced that kind of loneliness and immediately did something about it. He found time and a way to be alone with God the Father. In all things Christ is our example, as well as our Savior and Lord.

I haven't the slightest idea what the courts of heaven look like other than the fantastic descriptions God has given to us in the Bible. My imagination is not capable of conceiving the majestic splendor and breathtaking beauty that God has created as His special environment. I see evidences of it all around me in the beauty of this world and the magnitude of the universe, but that does not begin to offer the faintest clue as to what my Father's house is really like. I do know that I may always enter God's family room, for I am part of His family; and I know that one day I will walk the throne room as well as the gold-paved streets and the gigantic walls of that city.

I can well imagine that when Jesus in His humanity walked the hot, dusty streets of Israel, He often felt homesick for the flawless beauty He had known previously. And before every major happening in life, He turned His back on the crowds to be alone, locked in with God.

In Luke 9:18 we read, "And it came to pass, as He was alone praying. . . ." It came to pass. . . . Something happened when He prayed! And something will happen in our lives if we eagerly choose to use our moments alone to gather up all our resources in Jesus Christ through prayer. What most special thing does our heart long to have "come to pass"? Are there those in your family whom you long to see know the reality of Jesus Christ as Savior? Are you spending time alone with God on their behalf? We can never effectively talk to men about God until we first talk to God about men. It was as Jesus prayed alone that His disciples came to Him and first recognized Him as their Messiah.

I am sure that the peak experience of loneliness for Jesus occurred during the hours He suffered on the cross. There were jeering, screaming crowds pressing in on every side, but in His inner spirit He was alone. Only one disciple had followed Him all the way to Calvary, and that was John. From the cross Jesus spoke to him as He gave His mother into this faithful man's care. But even John could not have known or entered into the agony of Jesus as He prayed for those who drove spikes through His hands and feet: "Father, forgive them!" It was from His aloneness that *our* salvation was accomplished. The highest creativity of opening heavens' gigantic gates was totally accomplished that day so that "whosoever will" may walk in and enjoy God's life style all through eternity.

145

Are you alone and lonely? Thank God! You have a capacity to care about others, to know friendship, and to identify with people and with Jesus Christ. Reach out to Him and realize that when He shares your empty life, it will not be empty. As you begin to find Him filling your life with His, go quickly and share the exciting news with the loneliest person you can find. That person needs you. Don't wait to stockpile a lot of information — pass it on while it is fresh. We are not to be "Dead Sea Christians." That sea gathers the input of fresh flowing water from the Jordan River; but because it has no outlet, the waters cease to flow and it becomes a sea of death. The salt and mineral deposits are so heavy that fish cannot survive once they enter its restrictive confines.

I have heard many people say, "I would like to get acquainted with new neighbors" or "I wish I could communicate with my family, but I just don't know what to talk about or how to get them to talk to me." There are three primary reasons why people have little or no communication with each other:

(1) No one listens when they talk, and soon they simply stop talking.

(2) Personal insecurity and lack of self-value. They feel that what is meaningful to them may seem strange or foolish to someone else and perhaps it is better not to talk about the really important things. If one must talk, it may be safer to stick with the weather.

(3) Past criticism. At some point in the past when they have shared an idea, a dream, a hope, something that was important to them, others have criticized or attempted to change their mind about it, possibly in an effort to force

146

them to receive their own opinion. Criticism and attempts to change other people kills communication in any family. Perhaps you have had these things happen to you. If so, you can be more sympathetic and understanding of the needs of others.

When you begin helping others to become free to share their lives, you will find yourself on the front lines of real adventure in your personal life. Today I saw a miracle take place, and I believe it is one that can happen to anyone. I was with a group of sweet but lonely women. They had listened warmly and attentively to the session I had just given on loneliness. Then I took the list of favorite things you will find on pages 149, 150 and gave each of them a copy. I asked each woman to team up with one other woman she did not know personally, and using this sheet as a guideline, to spend twenty minutes getting to know her. The sheet of paper was merely a tool to assist in getting to know the other person. It was a twenty-minute opportunity to really share their lives. I also asked them at the end of that period of time to close their eyes and say simply, "Dear Jesus, I thank You for letting me meet ———— (fill in the name of their new friend) today. Amen."

When those ladies came back together to form the larger group, it was beautiful. They were excited about the fascinating persons with whom they had become so well acquainted in such a short time. One woman in her twenties had paired off with a lady in her sixties. They were radiant as they shared that they had discovered they both enjoyed the same things, had the same needs, and shared other common interests. Others had similar experiences: a lady in a wheelchair, a missionary mother of five who had raised her children

147

in Africa . . . the list is endless; but each one found someone special, when just minutes earlier most of them didn't even know the name of the women sitting near them. Many of those women are going to continue to develop this beautiful beginning, and life will be richer for many of them.

Would you like to be best friends with each person in your family? The following guide lists some "favorite things." Try filling it out on each person in your family. Don't guess at their favorite things; list them only if you are absolutely sure. Then when your family comes home, find a nice low-pressure time, possibly right after dinner, and let them know they are special to you — special enough that you really want to know the things they enjoy most. Talk with them as you would an exciting stranger. Be as sensitive and courteous, as listening and encouraging as you would be with a person whom you have never seen before. (Amazingly enough, we are far more considerate and polite to total strangers whom we may never see again than to those important people with whom we live each day!)

Remember that the guide is not important in itself but is a means to help you think of interesting things to talk about, to unlock the door of *their* interests and favorite things, to open communication channels free of criticism and any attempts to change the mind of the other person about *anything*. You may not get beyond the first question, "What is your favorite food?" You may even discover that you have been baking apple pies for thirty years when your husband prefers chocolate cream! You may have been stuffing yourself with chili because you think he likes chili, when he really loves fried chicken just as you do! You may find that his

148

favorite vacation is exactly what you have been wanting to do for years, but both of you have been caught in the trap of doing the traditional, whatever that may be.

But be prepared to find many surprises; and welcome them, for they are the exciting keys to that interesting stranger you have been eating and sleeping with for years. Don't you think it's about time to get acquainted with the real person behind the mask? Isn't it time to begin to be free to be yourself, to let them do the same, and to enjoy that marvelous freedom together? To paraphrase God's truth, it can be said, "They that water others are first watered themselves," and they that free others emotionally are first freed themselves. Together they can joyfully shout, "I am free to be me . . . the person God intended me to be!" Loneliness can become a dreary form of bondage and the introduction to depression, but the grim ogre of depression has an open door to a more beautiful person who knows the joy of:

SHARING FAVORITE THINGS

Favorite food _____
Favorite recreational activity or sport_____
Favorite state, town, country, or national park ____
Favorite holiday (and why you chose it) _____
How would you prefer to spend
    A day off _____
    A vacation _____
    Extra money _____
If you could begin a new career today, what would you choose to do?

_____

Is there any special thing you would like God to do in your life?

_____
_____
_____

Depression-Proof
Living

W HEN I was a child, my parents spoke often about the Great Depression, a time of bankruptcy for millions of people and companies. By contrast, the United States today is living in the most affluent life style the world has ever known, and yet our nation leads the world in its ratio of people who are suffering physical-spiritual-emotional depression.

In 1974 our nation had over nineteen million recorded cases of depression, and it was suspected that at least that many more were unrecorded. But the wild-fire epidemic of this condition had not yet begun! Two years later medical authorities contend that the figure has doubled. In other words, there are approximately forty million known depression sufferers, and there exists the strong possibility of at least that many more who have no medical records of treatment for that condition. Such a mass affliction would seem to necessitate a mass carrier or condition of susceptibility and exposure. A few days ago I asked our family physician if he had personally noted an increase of his patients' complaining of this particular problem. He replied, "June, I am convinced that everyone in the world is depressed at some point in his life, and frankly we are looking for workable solutions to this massive need."

I want to share with every person who is suffering from this monster depression the fabulous news that there are three simple, cost-free steps to freedom from depression available to anyone, anywhere, at any time that do not require a disruption of school, work, or any other positive involvement. It does not require any of the three known forms of treatment and can be done quickly and painlessly in the hallowed halls of a tiny one-room home or a hundred-room mansion. It is not a theoretical concept but one that I have shared in retreats and seminars with people from all backgrounds, many of whom have been a part of the medical profession, and at the same time sufferers from the problem they were attempting to treat in others. I have seen incredible transformations among these people and in some instances have returned by invitation to share additional insight in those annual meetings as many as five times. I have had the opportunity to actually talk with the people who have tried and enjoyed the new-found freedom of dynamic living.

I am not a doctor, but I am grateful for the findings

of those who are a part of the medical profession and for the privilege of drawing on these facts as a basis for understanding the need in so many lives today. I am told that there are three recognized major causes of depression and three currently established methods of treatment. They are as follows:

1. *Biological*

It has been recognized recently that certain biochemical changes take place in the brain-center of the severely depressed person. The question is raised, Did the chemistry of the body become imbalanced and cause the depression, or did the depression alter the body chemistry? Which is cause and which is effect? At any rate, a host of antidepressant drugs have been used to alter moods and to readjust chemistry.

The most recent treatment with a high success rate is lithium. It is not new; it was first discovered in 1817, but it was ignored and little understood until recent years. It is a natural product of the earth from which God made man, and now man is using it in a compound form to readjust body needs. The soft, silvery metal in its many forms is used in a wide variety of products from agriculture to nuclear production. In its medical application it requires trained supervision and rigid control. In the same way that insulin balances the chemistry of the diabetic, lithium balances depressive chemistry.

Not all researchers agree that depression stems from chemical imbalance, however. Some claim it is highly probable that it can be from a

2. *Genetic Origin*

It has been observed that when one person in a family suffers from depression, others in the same family are apt to do so too. But again the question appropriately arises, Is it genetic in origin, or is the spread due to the emotional impact of the sufferer on those with whom he shares the most intimate of family relationships?

Electro-convulsive therapy (ECT) has been a recognized form of treatment since the 1930s. It has been attacked at times but now seems to be regaining much of its waning popularity. Its chief advantages are the instant results as well as low cost.

For years the medical profession believed that depression was primarily a

3. *Mental-Emotional Condition*

Depression was believed to coincide with a sense of loss: the loss of a loved one, financial loss, or loss of status, respect, resources, or a sense of personal self-worth. Often it followed on the heel of disappointments involving children, marriage partners, or others who were close, especially if these people were involved in excesses of alcohol, drugs, or sexual immorality, or were runaways. These conditions seem to accentuate feelings of failure as a parent or partner and increase the possibility of depression.

The third popular method of treatment is psychotherapy. Of course, the medical profession does not necessarily match the basis of depression with the treatment as I have given it here. More often it seems to be done on an elimination basis: try one form of treatment, and if that is not effective, move on to another one.

If you are one of the millions of people who have suffered the nothingness and endless fears of depression, you are well aware of its characteristics and do not need anyone to rehearse them with you. You have struggled with the listless lack of desire to go anywhere, be with anyone, or do anything. You know that tears seemed to have tapped the ocean as their source, and at times even death would seem a relief.

But I Have News For You!

You are not "locked in" as I was in the department store. There is a way out — and up. You are not alone; and there is an abundant, exciting life ahead for you, free of depression, sorrow, sadness, and loneliness, if you are willing to take three simple steps!

These steps are literally cost-free and do not necessarily involve lithium or other drugs, although if you feel the need to continue an established program of medication temporarily you may certainly do so. A gradual tapering off may be to your advantage. It does not involve psychoanalysis or electro-convulsive treatment, but it does involve *you!*

Depression is a highly personal problem, and the solution is locked within the individual rather than drugs, equipment, or people trained to administer those forms of treatment. It is the person himself who has the key and the most reliable ability for quick, painless recovery.

There is one common denominator that I have found in every instance of depression. That key is fear. There are so many causes and types of fear, we cannot possibly do a detailed study of them all here; but we can consider the problem of basic root fear that in turn copes with all other forms and degrees of its family of fears. I believe that root to be the fear of personal inadequacy.

The things we fear are external objects on which the inward fear focuses and feeds. We may fear high places, tight enclosures, elevators, water, or a million other things; but they are not the cause. We get so involved in dealing with the leaves on the trees that we do not recognize the taproot that supports and anchors them all. Leaves die when the roots of the plant are severed; and we need not waste time or energy coping with individual de-leafing of fears, but rather cut the root that is its life line. We can spend years in counseling trying to identify leaves and ultimately discover the basic fact of feelings of personal inadequacy or an inability to cope with a person, place, or happening, or deeper still with ourself and God . . . with the reality of eternity.

We may use mood-changers, either stimulants or depressants, to change these inner feelings; but eventually they surface again when certain triggers are touched that bring them to the forefront of the mind. We may go through shock treatment to lessen the memory and temporarily alter thought patterns, but the root is unchanged. These are leaf-picking expeditions that bring temporary benefit to some people, and during that time of relief changes may take place that make a degree of help possible; but is that the ultimate answer? Is it what a person ideally longs to have happen in his or her life?

If not, then consider this simple fact: all the fears we mentioned a few paragraphs ago (fears of heights, tight enclosures, etc.) are all fears of personal inability to cope with that particular situation. We reason *unconsciously*, "What if I am trapped in this small room and cannot get out? . . . What if the plane doesn't make this flight safely; what will happen to me? . . . Am I prepared for the eternal results of the loss of my life?"

In the last three years I have flown one quarter of a

million miles, and I want you to know that every pilot I have traveled with has been the most *prayed-for* pilot in the air that day! I must confess I do not trust the pilots. Several of my personal friends are pilots with commercial airlines, and we have beautiful friendships. I love them, but I do not trust them with my life! I have never found any verse in the Bible that told me I must trust any person! In fact, Scripture tells me I am to love, to value, every person in the world; but I am commanded to trust God who alone controls my life now and eternally.

Neither do I trust the incredible capability and resources of the planes on which I fly. I have been in the control center of a Boeing 747 and was utterly overwhelmed at its complex instrumentation. But I don't trust it! I am grateful for and I appreciate and value the pilots, the crew, and the equipment; but I can only enjoy each flight after I have prayed and placed my faith in God. The God who is on the ground with me is the God of the sky, and it is wonderful to be a little closer to His fantastic home every time I am airborne.

A friend shared with me her fear of flying one day, so I shared with her my secret: *The God of the ground is the God of the clouds.* Soon after, she made her first flight to Hawaii. Another friend went to see her off and took her a small pocket camera. To calm her mounting fears as she sat in her window seat, she snapped a picture of the clouds during take-off. Later, when it was developed, she suddenly became aware of the cloud formation that outlined sharply the figure of Jesus Christ as it appeared in the clouds outside the window of the plane. She said, "June, He *is* God of the skies, the ground, and the keeper of my life! Flying is fun!"

She discovered an important secret: *We cannot*

fight fear. The sense of personal inadequacy to control or cope with a person or situation produces the feelings of fear, which releases a sudden surge of adrenalin into our physical system. Going back to my experience of being locked in the department store, I felt many physical changes. My heart was pounding; my throat felt like I was choking; it was difficult to speak; my knees were knocking; my hands were clammy and moist; and my pulse was racing. When I looked at my physical symptoms, my fear increased, which in turn released more adrenalin into my body chemistry, and my physical symptoms grew more intense. Suddenly my teeth were chattering; I felt nauseated; I was breathing harder than usual; and though I seldom perspire visibly, I'm sure I was then!

The human body is the most incredible chemistry plant the world has ever known, and it defies the combined research of the greatest minds and machinery to ever totally unfold its complex functions. It could only have been designed by an infallibly wise and loving God, for it has built-in defense systems against disease and danger that surpass any man-made radar equipment in the world. The chemistry balance is so precise that God has taken the time to lay out a perfect but relatively simply manual for operating our body plants to reject actual bacteria and damaging infectious diseases.

Medical research has announced that over 90 percent of all illness can be attributed to poor emotional attitudes, particularly those of fear, guilt, and bitterness. Those emotions change the chemistry of the body and cause the loss of the effective working of the chemical screen that God has designed to protect us from such exposure.

Consider the effects of fear on body chemistry. The body is designed to produce and release extra adrenalin in response to fear, to energize the body for physical defense in times of danger. I have a friend whose child was run over by a car, and the car actually stopped on the youngster's body. My friend had never been an exceptionally strong man, yet when fear clutched his mind and heart, as he saw his child beneath those wheels, instantly he picked up the rear of that car by himself to release the child.

Medical records are filled with similar accounts of people who have known the sudden surge of strength that enabled them to do amazing physical feats when fear flooded the chemistry plant with fuel. But by the same token, this positive power source does not have the discretion to recognize the difference between our moments of fear. It acts automatically and sends its resources to beef up the battle lines. We feel that surge as physical symptoms. If we then fear the *physical activity*, we add more fuel, which in turn *increases* the action. And that brings us to the first step in freedom from depression. It is simply to —

Set Your Emotions Free

We cannot and do not have to fight fear. The fear we feel is precisely that — a *feeling*. Feelings increase by focusing on that particular thing. To attempt to fight fear is to focus on it and then find it expanding to invade more and more areas of our life.

Have you ever had some "wise" friend tell you that you shouldn't be depressed or afraid? He may have even added that you should "straighten out," get it all together, and stop *feeling* that way. Yet he leaves out the all-important "how" to do it! I like a phrase used by Dr.

Claire Weeks of Sydney, Australia, who has written several books and has a TV series in Great Britain. The phrase is *"float past your fear."*

One day while in Israel, I rounded a bend in the road and there was the beautiful Sea of Galilee, calm and brilliantly blue under sunny skies. A small boat was just offshore and the figure of a person was lying back in the boat with hands crossed behind his head looking up at the occasional white puffs of clouds floating overhead. It was a picture of contentment and peace.

You and I do not have to go to Galilee to sail smoothly over the sea of adrenalin our body produces when Jesus shares the boat or vessel of our life with us. He is a tremendous navigator and captain as well. The waves may come, but they will roll on by, and we do not have to scramble to our feet and risk a sudden dunking in our little boat. He is firmly in control if we will hand Him the oars. It does not mean that the habit and reaction of our system that has gone on for years will never occur again, but it does mean that every time it occurs we can know and understand why we feel this way. We can turn off our emotional panic button and actually laugh at them, for they have been unmasked and we know them for what they are — just chemistry.

It is not *fighting* but *relaxing* that our tense nerves need. In 2 Chronicles 20:15 we find this tremendous statement, "Thus saith the LORD unto you, Be not afraid nor dismayed by reason of this great multitude; for the battle is not yours, but God's." And in verse 17: "Ye shall not need to fight in this battle: set yourselves, *stand ye still,* and see the salvation of the Lord"! It does not depend on you alone or what you can or cannot do, but what you will permit Jesus Christ to do *for* you.

How refreshing to sink softly into His arms of love. Try it when you go to bed tonight. Breathe deeply, exhale several times, and just turn loose and let your body find its own level. Don't try to force yourself to relax. Gently let your muscles go. Take your hands off of the control switch and find the deep comfort of simply resting. It is easy to take our little twinges much too seriously and fail to see that the very symptom we have feared is simply *the evidence that our body is performing wonderfully well!* Try thanking and praising God that you can *feel* all those little signs of its performance. It can become a wonderful assurance that the chemistry plant is producing according to its function! Thank God; don't fear the chemistry!

During recent months I have been recovering from a major automobile accident that cost me a number of pieces of physical equipment, among them a kneecap. At times I have found the necessary therapy to regain use of the damaged leg quite painful. One day as I was working with it, I suddenly realized I was fortunate to be able to feel the pain, for that was the very evidence that my body was working properly. People in graves cannot feel; those who are paralyzed or under heavy sedation for pain cannot feel. But I can *feel my body working.* I am alive, and I will walk well again. When I recognized this fact, an amazing thing began to happen. Suddenly my therapy was not as painful. Muscles, nerves, and fibers were relaxed and could perform the same routines much easier, and the pain was relieved. Thank God for the capacity to feel pain!

To thank and praise God is a form of worship or reverence, as Proverbs 10:27 states, "Reverence for God adds hours to each day; so how can the wicked [those who refuse to reverence God] expect a long,

161

good life?" (LB). Further on we read, "Gentle words cause life and health; griping brings discouragement. . . . When a man is gloomy, everything seems to go wrong; when he is cheerful, everything seems right! . . . A cheerful heart does good like medicine, but a broken spirit makes one sick" (Prov. 15:4,15; 17.22, LB). And then in Ecclesiastes 7:13 we are given this command: "See the way God does things and fall into line. Don't fight the facts of nature" (LB).

Nature is God's operational process for the maintenance of all things according to His design. There is a dynamic purpose for every operational process of our body. The capacity to fear is a positive and important asset. It triggers an early warning system that something in our life needs an adjustment. We feel hot rays of fire as fear flashes a warning signal, and we adjust; we draw back. We may see a speeding car plunging toward us and feel a sudden rise of fear that produces the adrenalin to propel us quickly out of its path.

People fear many experiences where the final result is unknown to them. A classic illustration of that type of fear is to awaken in the night with the sudden realization that they are being burglarized. Suddenly there is the choking or even paralyzing dread, "What if we can't cope? He may be armed. . . . We may be hurt. . . ." The "what ifs" that never happen cost us a lot of carefree living. The inability to cope with someone or something is life's professional stressmaker.

I have shared in my book *The God of the Impossible* that Hal and I were married accidentally — it was totally unplanned, and we were equally unprepared. We did not know how to cope with our own feelings, much less marriage, a child, and the onset and separation of World War II. As a result of our selfish immaturity, our first child was placed in a procession of boarding homes for the five most formative years of his life. When we began to wake up to living life instead of running from it, we brought our son home to live with us. He was a beautiful little stranger but had many emotional scars. I spent the next several years in various stages of anxiety, guilt, depression, and frustration. Any other adjectives you may choose to toss in would find their place in my experience. I did not know how to compensate for my past failure as a parent, nor did I know how to cope with the present needs of our son and myself.

It is destructive to tie one's self to the whipping post of guilt, sin, and past failure. Those things cannot be changed, but they can be forgiven. We will either run to the solution of forgiveness and a bright new future, or we will run from the problem and create many new ones to add to the boiling pot of fear and guilt that ultimately brews a deep-dish depression.

The opening pages of recorded history reveal Adam and Eve failing themselves and God even though they were in the Edenic environment of perfection, free of want or worry. Nevertheless, they chose to reject God's one command, given to protect them from all the negatives of life, and instead they substituted their desires for God's purpose. They chose to take what God had not given . . . the forbidden fruit always looks more tempting before we become locked in (even as did all the goodies in my department-store experience). Adam and Eve's disobedience to God can be summed up in three letters — s-i-n. No wonder Ecclesiastes says, "See the way God does things and fall into line. Don't fight the facts of nature" (or His operational process), for it is designed for our healthy, happy living.

To oppose it is to cause unhealthy, unhappy conditions. That's exactly what our first ancestors chose to do. They were fruit-snitchers, and they suffered the consequences of guilt.

Failure Plus Guilt Equal Fear

There is an important three-step progression in the development of becoming a free person. Past failures and feelings of inadequacy produce guilt, which in turn causes fear, and fear drives us to do one of two things: run from the situation or run to a solution. Adam and Eve ran from the problem they had made. But God did not leave them in hiding. He came to them and called them so that they might have an opportunity to see and face their failure and become freed from living with the depressive results. Adam admitted his sin and his feelings about his sin, although he quickly blamed Eve. He did not yet have the camouflage that we have developed today. He laid it out the way it was. He said, "I was afraid . . . I hid myself . . . I did eat [the fruit You forbid me to eat]" (Gen. 3:10-12).

There are many fascinating details about human behavior in those few short verses, but the only one that we will consider at this point is that failure to perform produces guilt, which in turn brings fear. We unconsciously conclude, "I am not adequate to cope with the demands of life. I wish I were, but I am not." This in itself can cause guilt, real or imaginary, whether it is a departure or violation of God's purpose for us, or imposed by our imperfect standards or those of other people, organizations, or society as a whole. Most anxious, nagging feelings grow out of this dim area, and we feel an impending sense of gloom or perhaps just the inability to expect anything good to happen to us: we don't deserve it; we have not earned it.

Guilt has only two solutions — punishment or forgiveness. God has not equipped any person mentally, physically, or spiritually to handle guilt and worry; but He has given us the ability to be aware of it and the privilege of doing something about it! When we attempt to live with guilt, our system breaks down under prolonged attacks. It is pointless to allow such feelings to linger, for God has provided His solution — that of forgiveness, not punishment. When Jesus Christ went voluntarily to His death on the cross, it was to offer Himself as the substitute for the full punishment for every failure, sin, and guilt. We can choose either to reject or gratefully accept His offer. In doing the latter we receive total pardon, which is God's plan and purpose. It is His desire that we exchange guilt for joyful freedom and the abundant life that Jesus Christ came to make available to us.

In the Book of John, Jesus said, "This is life eternal, that they might *know thee* the only true God, and Jesus Christ, whom thou hast sent" (17:3). The word *know* in Greek, the language in which the New Testament was originally written, is *ginosko* and is the same word used to describe the intimate relations of a man and woman who become one through marriage and ultimately in the sexual relationship. As two people have given themselves totally and without physical reservation to each other, and it is said they "know" each other, even so to have the eternal life of God is to know Him and His Son. The word carries not only the idea of relationship but also of appreciation and of having been approved. It is a word of continuance. We enter into the life of God through Jesus Christ and in doing so become one with Him; we are approved and appreciated, but we also return that approval and appreciation and move into a deeper development of *knowing* our God. By accepting Christ's love-gift of His life for our life, our debt is paid; and God never demands payment twice! We are debt-free before God!

Then what have we to fear? Listen to Romans 8:31:

> What can we ever say to such wonderful things as these? If God is on our side, who can ever be against us? Since he did not spare even his own Son for us but gave him up for us all, won't he also surely give us everything else? Who dares accuse us whom God has chosen for his own? Will God? No! He is the one who has forgiven us and given us right standing with himself (LB).

Because God forgives us and we are no longer guilty, it becomes possible for us to forgive ourselves and others. That which we cannot do the Jesus who lives in us is totally capable of doing for us.

About five years ago Corrie ten Boom and I were speakers for a women's retreat in the East. At that time Corrie shared this experience in forgiveness: Shortly after World War II one of the keepers of the Nazi concentration camp who had caused her and her family so much suffering and even death came to see her. He shared the news that he had received Christ as Savior since the close of the war and that he knew God had forgiven his crimes of inhumanity. But he also wanted to ask Corrie's forgiveness.

As the memories flooded her mind she said, "I can't forgive you." She was troubled about it but unable to change her feelings, so she finally went to an old friend who was a pastor. Wisely he said, "Corrie, on Sunday morning I pull the rope that rings the bells in my church. When I stop pulling the rope, the bells stop moving but the ding-dong goes on. You are troubled by the ding-dong of your memories. You cannot erase them and so you feel you cannot forgive; but the Jesus who lives in you can and does!"

How often we are plagued by the "ding-dong" of past experiences, especially hurts. We feel it is an indication that we cannot or have not forgiven ourselves or others. How good to remember that those things we cannot do on our own Jesus can and will do through and for us. We do not need to build a new destructive point of guilt and self-accusation by focusing on the "ding-dongs" of memory.

When we release the unwelcome equation of failure plus guilt equal fear, our emotional system can relax, and God has the freedom to flood our lives with His replacement trio of success, forgiveness, and faith. This beautiful new threesome sweeps us along to the second step in becoming free from depression.

Running Free

THE human body is wonderfully complex and interrelated. Anything that happens to any part of us affects the whole. As a sudden blow to a finger makes the stomach shrink back and causes a host of other sympathetic responses, each part of our being shares the pain or joy of other areas of our life. It is this inward impact of body, soul, and spirit on one another that brings us to the second stage of conquering depression: recognize and utilize the physical body as a valuable tool in the recovery and rebuilding processes of life.

Let me ask you a question: What did you see when

you looked in the mirror this morning immediately after getting up? How would you describe the creature that blinked back at you through the whiskers or the cold cream and curlers, as the case may be? I am sure you must have said, "Good morning, you *gorgeous* creature (or *handsome* fellow)!" You should have done so, for you are! You are of tremendous value. There are four words we should all repeat at least twenty times a day: "*I am of value.*" Try saying them now out loud: "I am of value." Sounds a little weak; let's put the emphasis on the am: "I *am* of value." Again: "I am of *value.*"

You are of value to God! If Jesus Christ lives in your physical body and shares everything you experience, then God has an investment in your life. You are His by creation and design, and you are His by purchase through giving His Son to die for you. You are of tremendous value. It is so easy to get caught on the treadmill of self-deprecation that we block the access to the investment of the tremendous talents and supernatural gifts God has given us. To belittle ourselves is to admit self-pity, and that is an insult to God and robbery to self.

We can't love others as we love ourselves if we are busy hating ourselves! To love is to value and that begins with *valuing ourselves*. Try telling God something *good* you see about yourself every morning before you start the day. If you'll do it, you're in for a brand-new life. Have you ever thanked God that He found you available to do little things — to write a letter to someone who needed to hear from you, fix a flat tire, bake cookies for a friend? Why don't you stop right now and tell God something you *appreciate* about yourself? Check out how you feel after you've told Him. Do you feel a little silly, released, relieved, surprised, or

170

shocked? Why? If God made you (and He did), don't you think He used good materials? If Jesus lives in you, don't you think He is capable of doing good things through you? How big is your God? Big enough to be praised?

Sometimes our adult logic is ridiculous! We know it is important for our children to have a good self-image, yet we wander deep in the valley of self-pity and defeat, hating ourselves and resenting others. Let's get it straight. God made us in His image for His glory, and it's about time we *expect* something worthwhile of ourselves. Negative feelings about self buries Jesus deeper in our lives than graveclothes ever did. It's time for resurrection! Time to build a habit of seeing not only our flaws and limitations but our good points too. Sight produces fear when it sees only impossibilities. By contrast, faith produces hope and peace for it focuses on God who is greater than self, sin, or Satan. Faith takes human risk and matches it with superhuman resources.

"God hath not given us the spirit of fear; but of power, and of love, and of a sound mind" (2 Tim. 1:7). Notice that it is God's order to cancel out destructive fear and replace it with constructive love. Not all people are easy to love, but to give love to others brings a healing expansion and release from selfishness into the life of one who will determine to love (value) the difficult ones.

Several years ago a Christian speaker said, "When you see that totally unlovable person coming toward you, lift your hands to Jesus. Ask Him to fill them with His love. Now let it flow through your arms and into your heart and mind. As that person draws near, hold out the hand that God has filled with love in a warm handclasp and release all of God's love through your fingertips to drench that person with the love of Jesus."

Soon after hearing that I had an opportunity to try it out. A new family moved into our neighborhood, and the woman made her rounds of the nearby houses each morning, turning her two small sons loose to "explore their new environment." From coffee cup to coffee cup she moved, while I mopped, waxed, and laundered. Those tiny boys seemed to find the most exciting adventures of all at my house, especially when I was away. One particular Sunday morning I arose early to get blackberry pies made before going to church. I had picked those berries in the scorching sun the day before and now the finished product was beautiful. These luscious pies waited on the counter-top ready for the guests who would be coming home to dinner with us. After our car rolled away, her boys went in. Later, when we came home, I found wall-to-wall pie. Drapes, off-white carpets, walls, and furniture were decorated in swirls of deep-toned reddish abstract art. It was a new expansion of finger painting.

I had just finished teaching a class on the subject of giving love! I took one look at my home and said, "Lord, I hate her!" Why lie? God knew my heart. I couldn't fool Him or myself, much less my watching family. Together we cleaned the house far quicker than I could clean my feelings. Self-pity, resentment, and anger filled my mind. We were going through a time of financial loss and could not afford to entertain, yet I had felt pushed into a situation of having several people for dinner. At least blackberries were free for the picking! I think my deep-down feelings were something like this, "Lord, here I am serving You, and You aren't doing Your best by me. We have no money, and yet I inherit the responsibility of feeding all these people. You know how hard I work, and look at that woman who does nothing all day long. Why didn't You at least take care of my house while I was busy teaching Your class and worshiping You?" Now if you asked me how I felt, I would never have told it that way. I would probably have unearthed my halo and said sacrificially, "We all have difficult days."

I was a deeply committed Christian who really loved Jesus Christ and wanted to love my neighbor . . . *if* she deserved it by doing what I thought she should do. But the time came when God enabled me to realize that it was her need of genuine, unconditional love that propelled her from house to house. Soon I began praying, "Give me Your love for her. Help me to see her and her potential as You see her." It even occurred to me that my home which had been given to God was *His* home, and if He could use a new temporary decor of berry tones, He should have the freedom to do so.

God did not cause those little rascals to invade our home, but He could use it for my benefit, her good, and His glory. And He did, when I was able to turn around and shed my self-pity. Self-pity is a substitute for God. It demands that God and others behave according to our desires instead of freeing them and ourselves to enjoy God's fabulous plan and purpose. Anytime we substitute self for God we are in line for wide-scale depression, for it is the total violation of God's preparational plan for our complete self.

No wonder God begins that incredibly powerful and practical verse in Timothy with the exchange of fear for love, power, and sound mind. Weak and debilitating emotions are transformed to assets. Human nature tries to protect itself, and when it feels it cannot,

173

there will be either a reaching out to the greater power of God to do so or inward fear and worry.

In recent surveys across the United States it was discovered that the number-one worry today is no longer centered around marriage relationships, finances, or how to control children. It is worry over possible physical, emotional, and mental illness. On the surface that seems surprising, but underneath it is to be expected. The fear of illness is a major threat, for it means lessened ability to cope with all other issues. It involves financial loss if work is halted; it causes accumulated work loads in the home as the laundry and cleaning pile up. It sponsors unwelcome doubts as to our competence to handle situations involving children. It may even bring us face to face with the major question of life after death. Are we prepared for that?

The Moneymaker of Mass Depression

Illness is big business today. It is one of the four top subjects for TV programing. Hospitals, emergency rescue squads, disease, and disaster flash constantly across the viewing screen of life via TV in our homes. In addition we are told that the average high-school graduate has already seen 18,000 murders committed in his home on TV. Do we need to ask why our society is violent today? Society has been programed, and we are the people who buy the products that pay to continue destructive programing. We can stop it anytime we choose to do so by simply boycotting the purchase of products that sponsor the demolition of the minds and emotions of our children as well as ourselves. But we don't.

Recently a seventy-two-year-old man fell on a downtown street. People stepped over and walked around his bleeding body before one man and his daughter stopped to help. Sadly, it was too late. The man died an hour later in the hospital. This tragedy did not happen in some primitive land or even New York City, but in our friendly Midwest! Television has programed us to dehumanized indifference as we see thousands of emergencies that are unreal; and when the real thing hits, we are emotionally frozen. We have seen it all before — on TV.

The mass depression in this country has been fostered and fed by the mass media, and we must wake up to the realization that we are on a suicide course of indifference — and we must do something about it!

Health for Today From the Past and the Future

Recently I was in Turkey studying ancient cultures. In the area of the church of Pergamum mentioned in the Book of Revelation, I visited the ruins of an enormous health center that had been built around a natural hot springs. While the health center was dedicated to medicine and emperor-worship, it also treated the total person, and entertainment was a major factor. The great theater permitted only comedies and happy plays to be presented, for the people realized the tremendous impact of entertainment on the total person. That was 2,000 years ago!

We can certainly borrow and benefit from the knowledge of the past, but exciting things are also happening in our present era of history. One of the most amazing and practical discoveries just now being unfolded is the incredible chemistry performances of the body and its effect upon our daily lives.

Men and women are constantly living with a repetitive monthly cycle that is controlled by that chemistry in varying degrees. Women are extremely aware that they do not feel the same way every day, but many don't know what causes the often radical shifts nor do they know what to do about them. The men in their lives are usually even more confused. This monthly chemical cycle is uniquely programed by the inner function of each individual's personal chemistry plant.

For a woman, the menstrual cycle is the gauge of changing chemistry that produces the full spectrum of emotional fluctuations. During the first week of the cycle, when estrogen is being produced on a large scale, the woman feels a sudden rise in physical energy, accompanied by an exhilarating sense of well-being and ability to cope. She is on an emotional and physical high; and because of the stoppage of emotional drain and guilt feelings, there is also the setting for a spiritual high. However, by the second week there is a leveling off; a stabilization takes place which causes it to be an ideal time to make long-range decisions.

In the third week begins the production of progesterone which counterbalances the estrogen. It is a neutralizing influence that prevents the body from exhausting its resources, while along with it comes a decrease in energy and the beginning of a sense of being unable to cope with situations.

Then the fourth week brings a sense of physical weariness, emotional turbulence, and feelings of inadequacy and defeat. Because the chemistry is not understood, feelings of failure as a wife and mother or as a career woman run high and self-image takes a nose dive. Often the unconscious verdict is reached, "I'm a failure. I hate myself. I've got to get away." The welcome mat is out to guilt, defeated thinking, and depression. It becomes easy to project the feelings of failure in the forms of criticism of husband and children or others. Yet the criticisms are simply a cry for assurance that even though her *feelings* have changed, her *relationship* has not.

But the message is not that clear to her husband. He may react by turning the assault around and adding to the fire unknowingly. He reasons, "What's wrong with *her*? She's crazy. I've always been this way, but she's not acting like herself. If this is the way it's going to be then count me out!" The "count me out" may only last long enough for a walk to allow time to cool down or a night spent at the club or with a friend. But it's a poor attempt at a solution that does not solve anything and may well encourage an increasing problem.

The Passing Parade

For those men who wondered what ever happened to the gal who seemed so happy a few days ago, I have good news. This is not a permanent condition unless you choose to make it so. There are three keys to eliminating most monthly conflicts. The first is to understand that this is not permanent, but a temporary situation. Your wife is the same delightful person she was the first week of the cycle. She has not grown lazy and fussy but needs to understand and adjust to this repetitive change in body chemistry. You can help her understand and control her actions and reactions with patience, understanding, and warm assurance that her relationship with you has not changed. It's your chance to be a hero, and in the final analysis you will benefit through a happier, calmer, and more stabilized home life, and you will also learn in the process to cope with the fluctuations in your own metabolism. However, most men do not experience change in body chemistry to the extent women do, and outwardly they do not react as strongly to their changes.

The second way in which you as a man can help your wife is in the important area of eating and sleeping properly. The fourth week is the worst possible time to indulge in sweet or salty snacks, and yet most women feel the desire for those very foods during this time. This ties in with the second step out of depression, for while one's body is a valuable tool in that recovery process, we will get out of it what we put into it.

Recently a national publication released the findings of an investigative board, stating that most foods advertised on TV were the poorest possible forms of food. Yet these advertisments influence a major portion of our spending. Most are high in sugar, fats, starch, and salt and encourage overweight, low energy, chemical imbalance, and higher susceptibility to disease. We must *forget* the corrosive "goodies" and get back to the basic nutritive fresh fruits and vegetables, dairy products, high protein and whole-grain foods. We need to get plenty of iron and vitamin B complex as well as other vitamins and minerals. Recent discoveries have been made in research with men and women in prisons who have had high patterns of hostility or depression. Those who have participated in a diet program such as I have just mentioned have found remarkable changes in attitudes and actions toward others. It is well known that both salt and sugar are contributing factors in depression.

Our bodies are valuable but not fragile. We need adequate rest without oversleeping. Excesses of even good things become destructive, and too much sleep can encourage a loss of interest and lack of involvement. Here are some little tips that can help anyone feel and look better: Practice breathing deeply a few times each day to get the fuel of oxygen into the lungs and bloodstream, and it will help burn up excess fat. Concentrate on stretching yourself! Stand tall as you reach for the ceiling with the top of your head; good posture allows the heart and lungs to work effectively unrestricted. Get outdoors for some part of each day. During times of stress and depression it is the nervous system that needs rest far more than the physical body, and sometimes a helpful change of pace can best be achieved by outdoor sports, recreation, or even such practical activity as yard work. It is valuable to set ourselves small tasks each day that can be accomplished as markers for our own encouragement, and gardening can provide a visible evidence of achievement and also serve as a great mood elevator.

I would like to encourage every couple to chart the monthly cycle on a calendar. Each month record the reactions to change as well as the physical high points; list when they begin and end. Understanding the fluctuations of the system and expecting predictable reactions frees us from the sometimes frightening uncertainty of our own reactions. We need not coddle ourselves but intelligently recognize that at certain times changes are the normal course of events.

Balancing the Bomb

I am deeply grateful to my friend Jean Lush and to many in the medical profession who have been working for some time on the theory of controlling the energy output during the high side of the cycle as a means of controlling the low side and achieving a more stable total month.

Medical science is just beginning to catch up with

biblical evidence. In the Bible we find countless illustrations of this concept. First Kings 18 and 19 paint a vivid picture of high adventure as Elijah spent the day on Israel's Mt. Carmel. He stood in direct confrontation with the entire nation, its king, and 450 prophets of their idol, Baal. Elijah had listened all day as the king's men had called in vain for their image to bring fire from heaven to consume their offering. As twilight softened the brassy sky that had given no rain for seven long years, Elijah spoke quietly to His God; and in instant response the flames leaped around the altar, consuming even the dust and stones. Even though the sky was cloudless, Elijah warned the king that rains were on the way; and as they hurried down the mountainside, the heavens poured torrents of water on a thirsty land.

It would seem logical that Elijah would be in a spiritual euphoria with such a tremendous victory before such a politically and socially elite audience. Not only were the king and the entire nation present, but all the prophets of Baal were killed in the demonstration! Elijah had known the incredible victory of being one man plus God against such odds. Yet there is no evidence of joy or satisfaction. Instead we find the mighty man on the mountain plunging deep into depression as he hears the second-hand report that Jezebel, the wife of the king, had threatened his life!

Leaving the high side of accomplishment behind, he ran to the wilderness where he collapsed under a juniper tree and begged God to let him die. The triumph had quickly faded under the tremors of weariness, as fear produced its frequent companion of escapism. However, God does not bring *extinction* into our lives but *expansion*. He fed and hovered over his weary servant, meeting his real need rather than his desire of the moment. Interestingly enough, Elijah showed no surprise or even gratitude for God's miraculous feeding. He simply took it for granted. After a time of rest he was fed again by the messenger of God and then told to continue his journey; however, this time it was not a flight in panic but a rendezvous with God at the sight where Moses had received the Ten Commandments from the Lord so long ago.

I do not know the amazing content of the food that Elijah received, but I do know that he was able to travel through that blistering arid region for forty days and nights without eating again! When he came to Mt. Sinai, where the sparkling springs offered water, the demands of the journey and the sense of struggling for survival were behind him. Unlike Moses, he chose a cave and no doubt would have buried himself there, much as the monks who live in the monastery there have isolated themselves from the mainstream of life today. But the God of Mt. Carmel is also the God of Sinai, and He did not stand outside His living quarters or turn His back. Instead He called Elijah out of the cave of despair: "What are you doing here, Elijah?"

Elijah replied, "I have worked very hard for the Lord God of the heavens; but the people of Israel have broken their covenant with you and torn down your altars and killed your prophets, and only I am left; and now they are trying to kill me, too" (1 Kings 19:10).

The great depression-maker of seeing only a limited self without resources to cope with the situation for the moment shut out the reality of God. Elijah has substituted the frustration and devastation of self-pity for the joy of praising God and the release of dynamic faith.

Elijah's problems did not start with Jezebel's threat

but when he changed his focus from God to self! He had made himself the substitute for God. Personal inadequacy must find a scapegoat . . . a substitute to blame. For Elijah it was his nation and its leadership. It sounds familiar today in the 1970s for it is easier to blame the leadership of the nation, the state, or the home than to accept personal responsibility to initiate change. Elijah's cry, like ours today, was, "The right (which is myself) is failing and the wrong (which happens to be those who do not join me) is succeeding." Elijah felt that he alone was right! He did not know or make any attempt to find out that there were actually more than seven thousand men in Israel who were completely true to God at the risk of their own lives. Later God would reveal this to Elijah. But at the moment Elijah's view is exactly the opposite of God's. Somehow Elijah must be made to see himself, the world, and God as God Himself knows it to be. The instruction class had just begun. " *'Go out and stand* before me on the mountain,' the Lord told him" (19:11). In other words, "Come out of your cave of self-pity, and stand on your two feet, and take a good look at *me,* and then measure *your circumstances* against what I will show you!" The Bible records that when God passed by a great wind followed in His wake that split the face of the mountain and broke open the rocks! What a wind! If a mountain could not stand against it, could one woman's foolish threats?

But the Bible is careful to add the comment that Elijah's confidence was not to be placed in the power of the wind, for God was not in the wind; He had already passed by. It was only an aftermath of His parade of power.

Next in this tremendous demonstration, the earth itself erupted in a fit of trembling that matched the

182

winds of heaven. No hydrogen or atomic bomb has yet been devised that can touch the magnitude of the power of an earthquake. Elijah recognized God as the God of heaven, for he had seen Him hold back the rains for seven years in a loving effort to draw His people back from the degradation of idolatry involving human sacrifice. In response to his prayer, he had seen God open the heavens and release rain to restore a thirsty earth. Elijah's God was the God of heaven, and now he saw Him proven in a most remarkable way as God of the earth. As the earth's convulsions settled down, fire raced in the footsteps of God like the blazing tail that follows a streaking comet.

Again God spoke to Elijah. It might have been something like this: "Oh, Elijah, tell me again, what was it you were running from? A woman's threat that you heard second-hand?" And perhaps God whispered, "I believe I brought you through the last confrontation with that problem. . . . It involved the whole nation under her control (for she certainly twisted Ahab around her little finger). . . . She had 450 of her prophets there, and now they're all dead. . . . Remember when you stood there facing them, one man alone . . . except for Me? *We were enough*, weren't we? Now why did you say you were here in the cave of depression?"

As Elijah heard the soft whisper of God's gentle voice, he hid his face but repeated his sad story of self-pity, criticism, and fear. O Elijah, who is your God? Aren't you the man who bravely told the entire nation to choose whom they would serve, Baal or God, and if God then to follow Him? Would you call running from a woman *following God?* Wasn't it God who fed your body and gave you rest? Wasn't it He who just demonstrated every practical reason to set your emotions free . . . to turn from fear to faith . . . to move from self-limitation to God's power source? Wasn't it He Himself who has taken His loving time to establish spiritual companionship with you when you needed it most? Years later His Son Jesus Christ would summarize that all-important fact in these words, "Without me you can do nothing" (John 15:5). I wonder if God shed a few tears that day over his beloved Elijah.

Then the Lord God told Elijah, "Go back by the desert road to Damascus, and when you arrive, anoint Hazael to be king of Syria. Then anoint Jehu . . . to be King of Israel, and anoint Elisha . . . to *replace you as my prophet*" (1 Kings 19:15,16, LB). Elijah was to go back to the source of his problem and crown a new king. Then God informs Elijah that he was never the only loyal man of God in Israel; there were over 7,000 that he was not aware of. But God knew them. . . . God's resources always exceed the need and often are totally unknown to us. Elijah was given great honor not because he was God's *only way* of accomplishing this tremendous job, but simply because God, for His own reasons, had chosen to give Elijah that prestigious place of favor and success.

How often we have taken God's choicest opportunities and read into them a similar "poor me" philosophy. Blessings become burdens when we tackle them without recognizing the presence and power of God. God accomplishes His work, but He chooses to share our fellowship and activity in doing so, intending it for our joy in walking with Him. Seldom does God walk the cost-free streets of ease; instead He moves into the jumbled alleys of needs. If we want only a padded chair of observation to watch the parade go by, we will

184

miss the high adventure of victory on the battlefront of human experience. We may choose to see life either through the eyes of "poor me" or through the eyes of our great God!

Elijah's enemies would be dethroned and defeated, but he himself would be replaced. "Anoint Elisha to be my prophet." Yet Elijah was yet to see a greater demonstration of God's might than any he had yet experienced. He would never know the threat of Jezebel's sword against his throat, for God would send His personal chariot to bring him home with a thrust of energy that our rocket program has not yet begun to imagine. There was no fanfare, no research of air currents, no great missile base . . . just a man and his God. A man who had known the depths of depression and fear as well as faith and courage, for whatever else he was, he was just a man whom God loved and for whom He had a purpose. And that is true of each of our lives today. Elijah's choices are our choices.

We can look at circumstances, people, places, and happenings against the background of our limitations or against the limitless resources and power of God. We can struggle in self-pity and fear or come forth out of the cave to stand before our God. The winds will blow, the earth will tremble, and we will feel the scorching breath of fiery circumstances. But we will also know that they can become reminders of the presence of a live God who frees us from ourselves. It is this God who set the precedent of searching us out in our needs even as He did with Adam, Elijah, and others throughout history.

Spiritual Companionship

It is God who teaches us that when we are most

depressed, we need spiritual companionship, for renewal begins with our spirit in harmony with His Spirit. It is there that we discover and set in motion the use of our fantastic supernatural gifts for that extra dimension of power and achievement. As new life flows from the control center of our being, it moves into our psyche, and joy and peace blend our temperaments and gifts so they can be expressed fully through the outer self, the body.

The God who has so designed this amazing self is also the One who has patterned the great triangle of spiritual companionship for those who have marriage partners. It is the husband and wife *under God* that forms this beautiful and powerful tower of strength.

I am told by a friend who is a contractor that the best geometric form for structures demanding great strength is the triangle. Many bridges and glass buildings feature this type of construction. But if the triangle suddenly is robbed of any one of its three equal sides, it has no strength at all. Our tripart selves are equally dependent upon a unity or harmony of the whole person. Whether we are men, women, infants, or senior citizens, we all without exception need spiritual companionship. Sadly, we try substitutes that do not balance our lives but accomplish just the opposite — a deteriorating imbalance. If we substitute endless hours of TV, radio, records, or endless other forms of input to the exclusion of spiritual food, those areas will become overfed, dyspeptic robbers. A healthy body and mind needs a healthy, well-balanced spiritual self. When God is missing in the human experience and the tripart relationship in the home does not exist, that home is ready to be put on the endangered species list. For the person who is not living with a marriage partner, God

Himself fuses that life with His great Trinity — Father, Son, and Holy Spirit — and so fulfills His tripart person — body, soul, and spirit.

This is the third step out of depression —

Establishing Spiritual Companionship

Total health depends on treating the total person. We can set our emotions free and reap the benefits. We can also utilize our physical bodies as a tremendous asset in the recovery process and do everything within our power to build healthy patterns for living. But the most important part of our total three-dimensional self, the spirit, cannot be overlooked and starved if we expect to live happy, fulfilled, depression-proof lives.

Too often we think of spiritual growth only in relationship to church attendance. It's important to worship, study, pray, give, and fellowship together with other people who know Jesus Christ as Savior and Lord. We are strengthened by the input and demonstration of others who share our faith in God. It is marvelous to attend Bible classes and participate in missionary outreach programs. But the ultimate quality of that outreach must flow from the inner relationship of the individual to Christ, and it is most powerfully revealed and demonstrated by our attitudes toward each other in our homes.

The home is the reality center of all living. God intends the home to be the visible living evidence of His presence in the world today. And He desires that our marriage partners have an important part in that spiritual companionship. We are all three-dimensional persons and cannot function at our best with only two-dimensional living. We choose to feed the physical body wisely for physical health. We care a great deal about the proper development of good mental and emotional health. But we especially need to allow time and opportunity for the spiritual feeding and growth of our eternal selves.

Today I went to the bank where I have a safety deposit box. There I looked at my small treasures: a handful of gold coins, a few pieces of jewelry — my special delights. Those things are all kept in a little box that has little value . . . a few dollars at the most. But it contains my treasures! One day I will take them out of that dull little container and take them home and put them in another container that is elaborately beautiful. It is the jewelry box I have in my home. This is a poor analogy, but it expresses the fact that our bodies are temporary but important containers to reveal the inner self. And one day God will call each of us forth from this body which will return to dust. But the eternal self — the soul and spirit — will be taken to God's home to receive its new form (or container) that will be totally perfect for conditions of eternal life with Him.

We are God's treasures — His most precious jewels, which are still in the polishing and refining processes. We are being shaped and buffed by circumstances and people, as well as places that seem narrow and difficult. But God's hand holds and hovers over us and draws us closer today than we were yesterday to that moment when our spiritual companionship will be completed on a face-to-face basis with Him. In the meantime it is His command in Ephesians 4:2,3 that holds a challenge we reach out to embrace: "Accept life with humility and patience, making allowances for each other because you love each other. Make it your aim to be at one in the Spirit, and you will inevitably be at peace with one another" (PHILLIPS). *Make it your aim!* Set a goal! It is amazing that we set job goals, educational, organizational, social, financial, recreational, and physical goals, but have no spiritual goals. God challenges us to the highest goal of all: "Make it your aim *to be at one in the Spirit.*" Then He promises, "You will inevitably be at peace with one another."

There were over 200,000 runaway wives and mothers and countless hundreds of thousands of runaway husbands, fathers, children, and teen-agers here in the United States in just three short months! These people were all running the wrong direction! Inward conflict, frustration, and guilt *drive us* and *divide us* internally. But God *leads* His dear children into deeper union. Spiritual companionship between a man and a woman built around their God is the strongest triangle in this world. It defies all the onslaughts of life and time and will continue into the next dimension of life as it shall be.

Ephesians 3:16,17,19-21 floods our spirit with peace and power: "I pray that out of the glorious richness of his resources he will enable you to know the strength of the Spirit's inner re-inforcement — that Christ may actually live in your hearts by your faith. . . . May you be filled through all your being with God himself. Now to him who by his power within us is able to do infinitely more than we ever dare to ask or imagine — to Him be glory . . ." (PHILLIPS). It is the glory of Jesus Himself who chases the last vestige of depression and paints our life with His glorious colors. No man or woman is ever born *prepared* for happy, successful marriage and life on whatever plane he or she has chosen to live. But victory and life at its best has been *prepaid* for all who come to Jesus, for it is available in Him who lived it for us. It is His transposed life within

189

us that is depression-proof. I have walked the shadows, and because I know their blackness, I appreciate the glorious "Sonlight" all the more. And when we have no physical companion, God becomes our spiritual companion in the supreme adventure of running free. Free from guilt, fear, self-pity, and all that would slow down or prevent the world from seeing Jesus today.

> Since we have such a huge crowd of men of faith watching us from the grandstands, let us strip off anything that slows us down or holds us back, and especially those sins that wrap themselves so tightly around our feet and trip us up; and let us run with patience the particular race that God has set before us. Keep your eyes on Jesus (Heb. 12:1,2 LB).